W9-BRM-093

Orange, Lavender & Figs

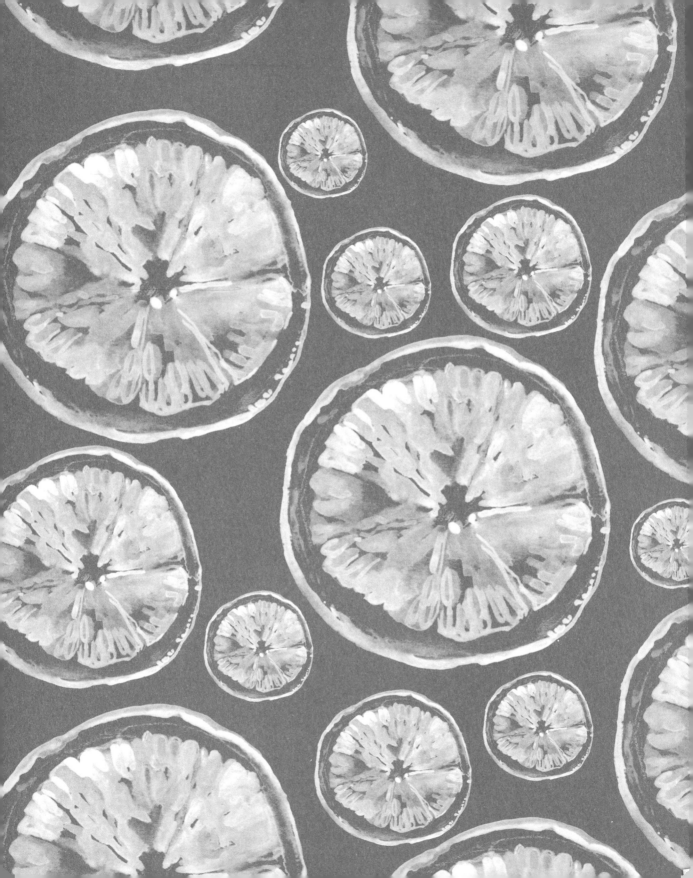

Orange, Lavender & Figs

DELICIOUSLY DIFFERENT RECIPES

FROM A PASSIONATE EATER

Fanny Slater

Foreword by Rachael Ray

RACHAEL RAY BOOKS

—

ATRIA

NEW YORK   LONDON   TORONTO   SYDNEY   NEW DELHI

ATRIA PAPERBACK

An Imprint of Simon & Schuster, Inc.

1230 Avenue of the Americas

New York, NY 10020

Copyright © 2016 by Fanny Slater

All rights reserved, including the right to reproduce this book or portions thereof in any form whatsoever. For information address Atria Books Subsidiary Rights Department, 1230 Avenue of the Americas, New York, NY 10020.

First Rachael Ray / Atria Paperback edition March 2016

RACHAEL RAY BOOKS / ATRIA PAPERBACK and colophon are trademarks of Simon & Schuster, Inc.

For information about special discounts for bulk purchases, please contact Simon & Schuster Special Sales at 1-866-506-1949 or business@simonandschuster.com.

The Simon & Schuster Speakers Bureau can bring authors to your live event. For more information or to book an event contact the Simon & Schuster Speakers Bureau at 1-866-248-3049 or visit our website at www.simonspeakers.com.

Interior design by Paul Dippolito

Food photography: Frances Janisch

Photograph on page 164 and 219: Tony Paixâo

Photograph on page 228: Paige Landsem

All other personal photographs courtesy of: Ra Elohim Remez and Jeffrey Slater

Manufactured in the United States of America

10 9 8 7 6 5 4 3 2 1

Library of Congress Cataloging-in-Publication Data is available.

ISBN 978-1-4767-9630-7

ISBN 978-1-4767-9631-4 (ebook)

To Mom, Dad, and Sarah—who encouraged my eccentricity, nourished my passion for food, and taught me how to hang socks on my ears.

Contents

Orange, Lavender & Figs

Foreword

by Rachael Ray

One of the things I really love about our daytime show is that our viewers can see so much of themselves in the work we do, and I truly believe that anyone can be a "Rachael Ray." We launched the Great American Cookbook Competition to give an incredible home cook the chance to share their favorite family recipes with everyone's families, and we were so excited when Fanny won. Food is at the center of my favorite childhood memories, and that's why from the start of the competition, I loved Fanny's cookbook concept, which evolved from the idea of recipes and flavors that "taste like childhood" to the finished product, *Orange, Lavender & Figs*. This cookbook serves up equal amounts of touching family memories, tasty dishes, and practical kitchen tips.

Fanny has already inspired me (and our show's viewers) with her unique voice, thoughtful reflections, and great recipes—now she'll be inspiring readers, too.

Oh, Hello, I Didn't See You Standing There

My great-grandma Fannie used to say, "If you ever put anything on backwards, like your pants, do not change or you'll be surprised."

I'm still not entirely sure what she meant by that, but I think it has something to do with life.

I'd like to jump right in and tackle the number one question that I know is on all of your minds. No, Fanny is not a nickname. It is my actual, real-life name. It is not short for anything, such as Fanstopher, Fantasia, or Fanelope—which ironically sounds like yet another body part. You can't have a suggestive, *cheeky* name like Fanny (see what I did there?) and not have a sense of humor about it.

As a kid, I proudly wore this name on the playground, and it helped me to develop a sense of independence and authority. Instead of resorting to tears when a callous group of boys would giggle at my expense, I would erupt into an animated spell of hysterical laughter, proving to them that I was either: a) recently released from child prison and not afraid to use my tuna sandwich as a weapon or b) courageous enough to laugh at myself.

My parents knew that my name alone would set me apart from the crowd, and thankfully they enthusiastically encouraged this behavior. So when I would trot down the stairs with my underpants on my head and a maraca in one hand, while some parents would have cried—mine would applaud.

Now, to address the other reason I've gathered you all here today.

One November morning I received a text from my nearly ninety-year-old grandmother that Rachael Ray was holding a national cookbook competition. "You never know," she wrote. I was at a place in my life where food had become front and center, and a spark inside of me was just itching for a light. I spent hours, days, weeks shaping my recipes, submission video, and essays into precision. My infinitely supportive boyfriend, Tony, taste-tested enough fig jam to sprout a stem. Being selected felt as likely as winning the lottery, but a voice inside me kept reinforcing that if I was to simply be myself—I couldn't lose. This intuitive tone in my head sounded an awful lot like a combination of my mom, my dad, my sister, and occasionally Britney Spears.

So I did exactly that. I entered the competition and did not hold back one iota of my quirky, food-centered self. I hit Send on my application and spent the next several weeks anxious and covered in goose bumps. I was beginning to think I had mono when suddenly one night, an unknown New York number rang through to my cell. It was Rebecca, a producer at *The Rachael Ray Show*. I had made the top twenty. Several weeks later, I had made the top ten.

On April 1 (of all days), the same number called again. This was it. The call I had been waiting for. Shaking and on the verge of tears, I teasingly shouted into the phone—at a person I assumed was Rebecca—that this had better not be an April Fool's joke. You can imagine my surprise when, through the other end of the line, came the frisky, familiar voice of Rachael Ray herself. *Note to future self: Don't yell at celebrities.* I had made the top five and was headed to the big city to compete for the grand prize of a cookbook contract. One month later, I was standing on the fateful stage of the finale with the only other remaining competitor. I had made the top two. Next to us was Rachael, and next to her—a photo of the winner hidden behind a curtain.

They say that when you die your entire life flashes before your eyes. As it turns out, that is also true for the moment that Rachael Ray is holding a velvet curtain over a giant photo of your face. Throughout the competition I had felt as if every second of my twenty-eight years had aligned to bring me there. Seconds before Rachael yanked the fabric and the winner was revealed, I squeezed my eyes shut and everything around me went blank. The encouraging voice suddenly reappeared in my head. I opened my eyes and was face-to-face with, well, my face. So as it turns out, the voice had been right all along. All I had to do was be myself, and I couldn't lose.

Stop crying. I'm not crying—you're crying.

Now that we're best friends, a bit about this book.

My life is a recipe composed of extraordinary culinary encounters. No, I did not trek through Thailand to feast on tamarind-covered ants, and I did not backpack through Canada to roast a moose on its own antlers. (Yes, I did just Google: "Where do moose live?") But I did learn how to smear crushed garlic onto chicken with my dad and wilt buttery rainbow chard with my mom. I have no idea what I learned in my second-grade math class, but I will never forget how to shape crab cakes. This remarkable bridge between food and childhood inspires my original recipes and defines my playful spirit in the kitchen.

Suspicious of anything that teetered into the world of formality, I chose to approach cooking in my own way. I absorbed every episode where my life intersected with food and allowed those moments to brand themselves onto my soul. As an adult I found that when familiar flavors reemerged, each mouthful would send me soaring backward to a plate from the past. *"Mmm,"* I would close my eyes and whisper, *"tastes like childhood."* This phrase became the concept I would eventually submit for Rachael's cookbook competition. Contestants were also asked to send three original recipes and an on-camera cooking demonstration. In my video—filmed in the very kitchen pictured on page 2, but starring several more teeth—I shared a special story of an English muffin breakfast sandwich. In my family, this treasured dish was dubbed the Tin Foil Surprise. I enhanced it with my Fanny flair by concocting a zesty jam featuring orange, lavender, and figs. This recipe opened the door that led me into the Great American Cookbook Competition. And since my great-grandma Fannie used to say, "Always go out the same door you came in"—I would also select it as the deciding dish of the final round.

As you hold these words in your hands, flip to the cover and run your fingers over the title of this book. These are the three ingredients that forever changed the course of my life. Never underestimate the fortitude of the *fruits* of your labor.

This cookbook is a celebration and reconnection of the stories, people, and ingredients that have guided me to this very page. It is a voyage through time, where I travel backward to the visceral memories of nourishment that have impacted my life. I then resurface in the present to unravel those edible moments and weave them back together into eclectic new dishes.

There is a children's book called *Sylvester and the Magic Pebble*. In this fable, a donkey from Oatsdale finds a magical rock and is granted three wishes. As this was my favorite bedtime tale—other than *Everyone Poops*, but that doesn't seem appropriate here—I'd like to tell you my three wishes for how this book will impact you.

First, it will make you unexpectedly laugh out loud. Along with cinnamon, I have seasoned this cookbook with humor so that it's more than just a collection of recipes. It's like a lunch date with a good friend—the kind who somehow ends up with hummus on her elbow and orders two beers before noon.

Second, it will grab ahold of you. Whether you grow your own microgreens or have no idea what a spatula looks like, I believe that each of you carries your very own anthology of rich food memories in every shape and form. I hope that my stories will remind you of your own and inspire you to pave your individual path to honor those experiences.

And third, this book will ignite your creativity in the kitchen. With simple techniques, whimsical ingredients, and an epicurean touch, these recipes are meant to guide ideas from the imagination to the plate. I have created this cookbook because I am inspired by the delicious, nostalgic components of my childhood. What inspires you? What will you create?

If you knew that the secret to life was simply to be yourself, how would you change the world?

You bought this book for one of two reasons. One, you saw the words "Rachael Ray" and were so excited about making short ribs in under 30 minutes that you skipped up to the checkout line without noticing that she didn't write this cookbook. Or two, you're a member of my family.

No matter the reason, I hope you have as wildly exciting a time reading this cookbook as I had writing it.

Cheers to childhood!

Fan

Fanfare Tips

The word "fanfare" refers to a short musical flourish typically played by trumpets. I had hoped to squeeze in several hand-drawn illustrations of brass instruments here—and some of my finest doodles (e.g., Calvin and Hobbes or Bullwinkle the Moose as Elvis)—but my editor shot that idea down before it even left my brain.

In my world *(Welcome! Don't forget your complimentary key chain!)* the word "fanfare" holds a very different meaning—as it is the fusion of my unique name (Fan) and my zealous passion for food (fare). When choosing a name for my Wilmington, North Carolina–based catering company, Fanfare was the only logical choice.

All of my catering experiences—from elegant private chef dinners to fun, interactive cooking classes—have helped me to hone my knack for presentation and enthusiasm for pairing. So, to share this expertise and pay homage to the Fanfare kitchen, I've dubbed the bonuses in this book Fanfare Tips.

You can expect to find presentation advice, where I pass along perspective I've absorbed in the catering world. Not just things like, "Don't lick the ice sculptures and never double dip when someone else is looking," but how a rich drizzle of balsamic can add depth and a striking contrast of colors to an average plate.

You will run into Flippidy-Doo's, which is a word I invented for when one recipe can be the inspiration for another brand-new recipe. For example, if you find yourself with leftover Sweet Potato Pumpkin Latkes (page 16), a Flippidy-Doo advises you to stack them atop a mountain of vinaigrette-dressed mixed greens. And which vinaigrette in the book will go best, you ask? The Flippidy-Doo will guide you there.

There are also suggested flavor change-ups, ingredient substitutions, and tips on timing. Occasionally you'll even stumble upon wine pairings, where I explain, for example, what Rieslings and pears have in common. These helpful hints will also teach you important life lessons like, "You can never have too much fig jam."

It's going to be a tasty ride.

Chapter 1

Rise and Scramble

Each morning I leap out of bed for one very specific reason: It's time to eat again. This sunrise section starts off your day with a series of brunch-style recipes that are meant to be slowly savored and served with a side of mimosa.

The Tin Foil Surprise

Here is what I learned on the first day of school: Punctuality is not my strong-point.

It's nearly 8:00 a.m., and I am upstairs doodling inside my latest volume of *Calvin and Hobbes*. I hear my dad's voice and race to the car. In a speedy attempt to fuel me with a nourishing, homemade breakfast, he hands me a tin foil—wrapped creation. Inside: a savory symphony of creamy scrambled eggs, gooey sharp cheddar, and woody sage sandwiched in a buttery toasted English muffin. As I peel back the shiny wrapper, with a wink in his eye he turns to the backseat and says, "What did you get?" That's how the Tin Foil Surprise was born and the family ritual began.

A few words on English muffins.

English muffins have always held a special place in my heart. There's something comforting about them, like a soup crock or an old pair of sweatpants that the elastic has snapped on. For my sister and me, the nutty smell of these yeasty muffins browning in the toaster was our daily alarm clock. The pop of butter sizzling from a stream of eggs was the five-minute signal. The clang of drawers opening and closing as my dad searched for the cheese grater was the one-minute warning. I dreaded everything about school, but looked forward to that spectacular sandwich every morning.

Life moved forward, and the foil-enclosed packet followed me—as I would construct it for myself on momentous mornings like the first day of college, a job interview, or a cross-country move. One November day I received a text from my grandmother that Rachael Ray was holding a cookbook competition and that I should give it a shot. For my three-minute video demonstration, I chose the most powerfully influential—yet simple—dish of my life and tweaked it with an orange lavender fig jam. I called it the Tin Foil Surprise.

Two traditions began on my first day of school: the Tin Foil Surprise breakfast sandwich and the "show your grade on your fingers" photo. Here my sister, Sarah, displays that she is entering fourth grade—while I present a make-believe microphone and practice for my future career as a television host. Academia and I were clearly off to a running start.

Nearly one thousand contestants and six months later, I was in the top two and faced with the final challenge. I rifled through the pages of my internal recipe book, but nothing put my mind at ease. Several nights before flying back to New York for the conclusion of the competition, my dad suggested that I end where I had begun. A sudden calm fell over me and I said, "If the biggest moment of my life is relying on an English muffin—I think everything is going to be okay."

★ **First-Prize Breakfast Sandwich with Orange Lavender Fig Jam** (page 12): I have tinkered with my nostalgic nosh by adding a citrusy, floral fig jam, tangy Taleggio, and peppery arugula for a crunchy bite.

First-Prize Breakfast Sandwich with Orange Lavender Fig Jam

SERVES 4

This exceptional breakfast creation marries fluffy, omelet-style eggs and floral fig jam with buttery Taleggio cheese and crispy English muffins. For those who linger at the Sunday brunch table, this sweet and savory sandwich makes for an extraordinary sit-down delight. For busy weekday mornings, break out the tin foil and wrap it up for easy on-the-go eating.

½ cup Orange Lavender Fig Jam (page 217)
6 large eggs
½ teaspoon kosher salt
¼ teaspoon coarse black pepper

4 English muffins, split in half
1½ tablespoons unsalted butter
8 ounces Taleggio cheese, rind removed and sliced
1 cup baby arugula

Make the Orange Lavender Fig Jam and place it in the fridge to cool down while you prepare the rest of the ingredients.

Position a rack 4 to 6 inches from the heat and preheat the oven to broil.

In a bowl, whisk the eggs with the salt and pepper. Toast the English muffins until golden brown and set aside.

In a large nonstick skillet, heat the butter over medium-high heat. When the butter begins to foam and sizzle, pour the eggs into the pan. As the bottom begins to cook, lift up the outside of the eggs with a heatproof spatula so that the runny center flows to the sides of the pan. When the bottom is fully cooked—about 30 seconds—carefully flip the eggs so that they're now top-side down. If you're not comfortable flipping the eggs, scramble them with the spatula until soft and fluffy. Immediately remove the eggs from the heat and divide into 4 portions.

Spread all 8 toasted English muffin halves with fig jam. Top 4 of the halves with even portions of scrambled egg and Taleggio, and place them on a baking sheet. Broil until the cheese is melted, about 45 seconds. Top the melted cheese with arugula and the other half of the English muffin.

Fanfare Tip

To achieve a tasty meal on a hectic morning, think ahead. Prepare this sandwich the night before, wrap it in foil, and refrigerate. When you roll out of bed, head to the kitchen and pop the package into a 350°F oven. Twenty minutes later and you'll be on your way with a breakfast to boast about.

Lavender, Kale, and Pistachio Smoothie

I remember when smoothies came only in pink. Next thing we all knew, the green drink craze swarmed the nation and the inside of everyone's tumbler looked like Kermit the Frog's unfortunate accident. Well, I'm here to tell you: Trust the trend. You'll have no idea you're slurping down a nutrient-rich veggie. This cold concoction tastes more like smooth, fluffy, vanilla-y air. I love air.

Note: No Muppets were harmed in the making of this drink.

1 cup vanilla almond milk or vanilla soy milk
Juice of 1 orange
¼ cup blueberry Greek yogurt (or your favorite flavor)
¼ cup pistachios, dry-toasted in a skillet over medium-low heat for 5 minutes

1 banana, roughly chopped
1 tablespoon chopped fresh lavender or ½ teaspoon dried
1½ tablespoons honey
6 large kale leaves, ribs removed and roughly chopped
1 to 2 cups crushed ice

In a high-powered blender, pulse the almond milk, orange juice, yogurt, pistachios, banana, lavender, honey, kale, and 1 cup of the ice until very frothy and smooth.

Taste for sweetness and if needed, add more honey. For an icier smoothie, add the remaining ice and pulse until thoroughly blended.

Fanfare Tip

High-powered blenders (like Vitamix) are ideal for blasting the greens in these frosty drinks. If you're working with an old-school model, here's what to do. Start with the liquids on the bottom and pile in the remaining ingredients except for the ice. Blend for 2 to 3 minutes straight until the leaves are very thoroughly blended into the mix. Once you've got a luscious, velvety texture— toss in the ice and zip away until chilled.

Extra Friggin' Good

This is the true story of Fanny Slater's catering business.

Well, the first one at least.

My mom had been making blended breakfasts for as long as I could remember. As I would be piling mounds of peanut butter onto a single piece of toast (see photo on page 187), I would stare in astonishment as she dropped everything from arugula to avocados into the blender. A splash of mango nectar here, a drop of coconut milk there. She was a ferociously fearless frothy drink artist, and I wanted in on the idea. So one summer, I turned the luggage cart at our coastal vacation rental into my very first business.

Aptly named EFG—Extra Friggin' Good—my smoothie mobile made its debut into the world. I wandered from door to door offering custom-made juice creations and the opportunity for vacationers to sample food from a strange adolescent youngster in her awkward phase. I wore my most professional attire: an oversize Special Olympics volunteer T-shirt and a pair of Umbros. Looking back, I applaud myself for my unique fashion sense, as I had a spirited determination to stand out. My menu was a handwritten poster board I had taped to the side of my portable enterprise. I did not accept checks.

And then I sold one.

You'd think this is the part where I finish telling the story, but that's it.

I sold one. Just the one.

Today, I experiment with all kinds of untraditional icy creations, and I owe that to my mom, who taught me boldness at the blender. I adore the floral notes of fresh herbs or the nutty aroma of toasted oats. I swap soy milk for almond milk, and blueberries for blueberry Greek yogurt. I have investigated smoothies

I would like to note for the record that I was wearing the fashion-forward outfit (mentioned on the opposite page) in 1998, when I met Britney Spears (following a thirteen-hour wait in a hotel lobby with my incredibly patient dad). Britney, if you're reading this, I appreciated your sincere kindness despite my extraordinary ensemble, and I hope you know I just couldn't find my tube top that day. Also, I am now thirty years old and still your biggest fan.

from top to bottom and here is my conclusion: If it's a flavor you love, you can't go wrong. I have also learned that it's not about how you dress yourself, but how you dress your plate that matters. Or in this case, your cup.

To the kind lady at Wrightsville Beach who bought that smoothie from me back in 1996: Your two dollars didn't pay for my braces, or my new pair of glasses, or even the toy I would purchase the following day for our black Persian cat, Zoro. But you certainly helped shape my entrepreneurial skills at an early age. I raise my smoothie glass to you.

★ **Lavender, Kale, and Pistachio Smoothie** (page 13): I buzz vibrant greens with fresh sweet orange, creamy almond milk, and fragrant lavender for a slurpable morning pick-me-up.

Sweet Potato Pumpkin Latkes with Maple Mascarpone Cream

You don't have to celebrate Hanukkah to experience these crispy pancakes. Savory and sweet all in one bite, these patties are laced with pumpkin and oniony leeks and topped with a luscious maple-infused drizzle. Mazel tov to mascarpone!

Platter up these seasonal latkes for your next fall fiesta and be the hit of the holiday party. Or if all else fails, spin the dreidel and turn it into a drinking game. Whatever floats your haroset.

1 tablespoon olive oil

2 leeks, white and light green parts only, diced

Kosher salt and coarse black pepper

2 pounds sweet potatoes

½ cup canned pumpkin puree or 1 cup diced roasted pumpkin

1 teaspoon minced fresh ginger

¼ teaspoon ground coriander

1 tablespoon light or dark brown sugar

¼ teaspoon ground cinnamon

2 large eggs, beaten

¼ cup flour

1 teaspoon baking powder

About 1 cup neutral oil (such as vegetable, grapeseed, or sunflower), for pan-frying

Maple Mascarpone Cream (recipe follows)

In a medium skillet, heat the olive oil over medium heat. Add the leeks and season with salt and pepper. Cook, stirring occasionally, until the leeks become translucent, about 5 minutes. Cool to room temperature.

Peel the sweet potatoes and grate on the large holes of a box grater. Place the shreds in cheesecloth or a kitchen towel. Squeeze out as much moisture as possible and then transfer the shreds to a large bowl.

Flippidy-Doo

Lotta latke leftovers? Use the extras as toppers for a hearty mixed greens salad doused in Orange Maple Vinaigrette (page 174).

Into the bowl with the potatoes, add the sautéed leeks, pumpkin, ginger, coriander, brown sugar, cinnamon, eggs, flour, baking powder, 1 teaspoon salt, and ½ teaspoon pepper and toss to combine.

In a large nonstick skillet, heat 2 tablespoons of the neutral oil over medium heat. Without crowding the pan, drop about 2 tablespoons of batter at a time into the oil. Sauté each latke, adding more oil as necessary, until golden brown and crispy, 2 to 4 minutes per side. Transfer the latkes to paper towels to drain and immediately sprinkle them with salt.

Plate the latkes, 3 per person, and serve each portion with a heaping tablespoon of Maple Mascarpone Cream.

Maple Mascarpone Cream

MAKES 1½ CUPS

1 cup mascarpone
⅓ cup maple syrup
½ teaspoon grated orange zest

1 tablespoon orange juice
Pinch of kosher salt

In a small bowl, whisk together the mascarpone, maple syrup, orange zest, orange juice, and salt.

The Hanukkah Socks

My friends were always jealous that I got to celebrate Hanukkah and collect eight nights of presents.

They were wrong.

A typical Hanukkah in our house meant that I would first receive a dazzling pair of socks—and the remaining evenings, a pat on the head for not knocking over the menorah. Of course over the years I received many wonderful gifts from my family, but it was never about tearing open boxes and exchanging material things. Well, unless that thing was a Game Boy. The tradition of lighting the candles, eating a nourishing meal, and being together was what mattered most. Although there was that one year I hid a Christmas tree in my closet and surrounded it with various items that I gift wrapped—a loaf of bread, my sister's alarm clock—from around our house. I was fifteen and desperately wanted to meet Santa Claus.

I digress.

As a child, I was privileged to experience many blessings related to growing up in a Jewish family. (No, Mom and Dad, I'm not referring to the drum set I received for my Bat Mitzvah, although that was a pretty spectacular wish-come-true.) On special occasions like Hanukkah I was fortunate to witness my dad produce his signature homemade potato latkes. The crisp, salty sting of grated potatoes splashing into a pool of oil is a sensation that zips me back to childhood. Captivated by the aroma—but using my dad as a shield against arbitrary spews of scorching grease—I would carefully lean around him as he released a spoonful of creamy potato shreds into a glistening pan. With a wide spatula and a flick of his wrist, he would toss them top-side down, revealing a crispy patchwork of wispy golden brown slivers. These miniature sublime pancakes were a thing of beauty, the perfect marriage of crunchy and fluffy, earthy and ethereal, and we gobbled them down faster than he could wrestle the lid off the cinnamon applesauce.

The delighted faces of two Jewish girls stuffed with love and latkes. Here, we are just moments away from being the proud owners of at least four new pairs of fuzzy socks.

Another delicious Hanukkah tradition we enjoyed as a family was my dad's heavenly homemade challah. I remember braiding, brushing, and baking this beautiful bread from scratch under his watchful eye. I can still see my dad in a flour-covered apron, schooling my first-grade class on layering and twisting delicate strands of velvety dough. I played mini sous chef and adored the yeasty tang under my fingertips. To finish we would paint the loaf with a milky sheen of liquid egg and scatter poppy seeds over top. At home our challah was playful, whimsical in shape, and permeated with bright orange zest and warm, herbal cardamom or brown sugar and spicy cinnamon.

Who needs eight nights of presents when you have a lifetime of unforgettable, edible memories?

★ **Sweet Potato Pumpkin Latkes with Maple Mascarpone Cream** (page 16): As a play on the sweet and savory latkes and applesauce from my childhood, I infuse sweet potato pancakes with salty leeks and earthy pumpkin and top them with a rich maple cream.

★ **Sweet Challah Grilled Cheese with Maple, Pear, and Taleggio** (page 202): I split the eggy bread down the middle, stuff it with Taleggio and juicy pears, and parade this decadent grilled cheese as dessert.

Dilled Zucchini and Feta Fritters

These patties belong under the category "you can never have too much of a good thing." Brilliant for breakfast, brunch, lunch, or dinner, you can eat these savory snacks six ways from Sunday . . . to . . . next Sunday. In the morning, top with a runny fried egg. At night, pair with a bright frisée salad. At midnight, serve alongside whiskey on the rocks with a side of *Seinfeld*.

2 pounds zucchini, grated
Kosher salt and coarse black pepper
1 tablespoon olive oil
1 medium shallot, minced
2 large eggs, beaten
¼ cup chopped fresh dill
1 teaspoon baking powder
¼ teaspoon ground cumin

1 teaspoon grated lemon zest
½ cup crumbled feta cheese
½ cup all-purpose flour
About 1 cup neutral oil (such as vegetable, grapeseed, or sunflower), for pan-frying
Minted Yogurt Sauce (recipe follows)

Place the grated zucchini in a colander in the sink and sprinkle generously with salt. Let this sit for 15 to 20 minutes and then place the shreds in cheesecloth or a kitchen towel and squeeze out the excess water. Place the zucchini in a large bowl.

In a small skillet, heat the olive oil over medium heat. Add the shallot, season with salt and pepper, and cook until translucent, about 3 minutes. Let the shallot cool to room temperature and then add it to the bowl with the zucchini.

To the same bowl, add the eggs, dill, baking powder, cumin, lemon zest, feta, flour, 1 teaspoon salt, and ½ teaspoon pepper and toss to combine.

In a large skillet, heat 2 tablespoons of the neutral oil over medium heat. Without crowding the pan, drop about 2 tablespoons of batter at a time into the oil. Cook each fritter, adding more oil as necessary, until golden brown and crispy, 2 to 4 minutes per side. Transfer the cooked fritters to paper towels to drain.

Serve with Minted Yogurt Sauce.

Minted Yogurt Sauce

MAKES 1 CUP

¾ cup plain Greek yogurt
1 tablespoon chopped fresh mint
1 tablespoon fresh lemon juice

1 tablespoon honey
Kosher salt and coarse black pepper

In a small bowl, whisk together the yogurt, mint, lemon juice, and honey. Season to taste with salt and pepper.

Fanfare Tip

Pair these dill-infused patties with a citrusy, floral Riesling to complement the bright lemon zest.

Pee-wee's Potato House

This is not a story about Pee-wee Herman, but in fact a delightful tale about breakfast, where the moral is a recipe for peewee potatoes. (I can see how you'd be confused.)

Each summer when I was a kid, my family would pack our bathing suits, a bag of art supplies, an Enya CD, and the contents of our kitchen into a cherry tomato—colored Volvo station wagon.

Who can say where the road goes?

Well, for us, it was to Wrightsville Beach, North Carolina.

It's no surprise that as an adult I ended up choosing to settle in this coastal town, as many of my favorite childhood memories are from our family vacations

1997: Waiting our turn for a table at the home of my favorite breakfast potatoes—Causeway Café in Wrightsville Beach, North Carolina. Not pictured: the rest of my motorcycle gang.

at Wrightsville Beach. Other than the fantastic homemade meals we enjoyed on our seaside balcony, when it came to food there was nothing I looked forward to more than our ritual breakfast excursion to Causeway Café. One step inside the noisy restaurant and we were immediately flooded with the smoky scent of sizzling bacon and the amber aroma of maple syrup. I remember sticky, overflowing mugs of hot chocolate. I remember infinite stacks of honey-colored malted pancakes studded with everything from bananas to M&M's. But most of all, I remember the home fries: a buttery mix of fluffy and crunchy golden potato bits that had been seared to perfection on a blissfully gleaming flattop.

When our sunshine-filled weeks at the beach were up, we returned to Raleigh, where I would resort to potato plan B. Just ten minutes down the road was Brigs Restaurant, a local breakfast bistro with every early-morning craving I could dream of. Once a week, my mom would bring me there after school to linger over a large order of their crispy breakfast potatoes, redolent with slivered onions and smoky paprika. They tasted like a warm hug from a familiar friend—whose name was Causeway and who lived two hours away.

Now that I'm all grown up(ish), I skip the hour-long wait at the local diner and invite the comforting power of potatoes into my own kitchen. Caramelized *this*, roasted *that*, and whatever fresh herbs I can get my hands on. I begin with the memories of the starches that have stimulated my palate, and then let my imagination take it from there.

★ **Spicy Smashed Peewee Potatoes with Caramelized Shallots** (page 24): I skip the dicing by opting for tiny taters and bring a hint of savory sweetness with slow-cooked shallots.

Spicy Smashed Peewee Potatoes with Caramelized Shallots

SERVES 4

Kick off your kicks and slide on your slippers because your new Sunday brunch spot is right here at home. These are the hash browns you've been craving all week: crispy crushed baby potatoes tangled with sweet caramelized shallots and flecked with heat.

2 pounds peewee or fingerling potatoes
1 tablespoon unsalted butter
1 medium shallot, thinly sliced
1 teaspoon honey
Kosher salt and coarse black pepper
2 tablespoons neutral oil (such as vegetable, grapeseed, or sunflower)

1 teaspoon paprika
½ teaspoon red pepper flakes
¼ teaspoon cayenne pepper
1 medium clove garlic, minced
2 tablespoons chopped fresh herbs (such as oregano, thyme, or a mix)

In a large pot, combine the potatoes with enough cold salted water to cover. Bring to a boil over high heat, reduce to a simmer, and cook until the potatoes are knife-tender, 8 to 10 minutes. Drain and set aside until cool enough to handle. Halve any of the large potatoes.

In a small skillet, heat the butter over medium-low heat. Add the shallot and honey and cook, stirring occasionally, until the shallots are golden and caramelized, 15 to 20 minutes. Season with a pinch each of salt and pepper.

In a large skillet, heat the neutral oil over medium-high heat. Add the potatoes, paprika, pepper flakes, cayenne, and ½ teaspoon each salt and black pepper and cook for 2 minutes.

Flippidy-Doo

Try these taters any time of day. Dance them over to the dinner table, as they make an excellent side for Madeira Chicken with Tarragon and Shiitakes (page 124).

Using a potato masher, gently push down on some of the potatoes so they split but don't completely break apart.

Turn the heat down to medium and add the garlic, chopped herbs, and caramelized shallots. Cook, stirring occasionally, until the garlic has melted into the potatoes, about 3 minutes. Season to taste with salt and pepper.

Fanfare Tips

- No luck finding peewees or fingerlings? No worries. Go for Yukon Gold or red potatoes instead and cut them into hash brown–size pieces. Achieving the potato's crisp exterior and fluffy center isn't dependent on the variety—it's all in the parboiling. The quick precook ensures a creamy interior and crunchy outer layer.

- Timing is everything. If you're going for the breakfast "works," you want everything ready ahead of time so that your hot, fresh eggs are the last thing on the plate. Prepare the potatoes, brew the coffee, slice the fruit, stack the forks. As for the potatoes, pop them in a warm oven until you're ready to ring the breakfast bell. These should be done long before the eggs hit the pan.

Apple Chicken Sausage, Wild Mushroom, and Fontina Frittata

SERVES 4

You don't need an omelet station to enthuse your friends for that Sunday brunch party you're now wishing you had never offered to host. Three words: Bloody Mary bar. Okay, one more word: frittata. A frittata is a completely customizable, crustless quiche that cooks in the pan and finishes under the broiler. Prepare yourself for roaring applause as you slide this fluffy, golden brown, pizza-esque casserole out of the oven. Sharp fontina cheese, earthy mushrooms, and sweet chicken sausage come together to create an impressive one-pan breakfast that will finally convince your friends you're fancy. Vodka also helps.

2½ tablespoons unsalted butter
1 medium sweet onion, thinly sliced
 (about 1 cup)
1 teaspoon honey
¾ teaspoon kosher salt
¾ teaspoon coarse black pepper
2 tablespoons olive oil

½ pound fully cooked apple chicken
 sausage links
1 cup shiitake mushroom ★
 caps, sliced
6 large eggs
2 tablespoons half-and-half
1 cup grated fontina cheese
1 tablespoon chopped fresh thyme

In a medium skillet, heat 1 tablespoon of the butter over low heat. Add the onion and honey and cook, stirring occasionally, until the onions are golden and caramelized, 20 to 25 minutes. Season with ¼ teaspoon of the salt and ¼ teaspoon of the pepper. While the onions are caramelizing, move on to the chicken sausage.

★ One drizzly Manoa morning in Hawaii, my sister brought me to Morning Glass—the neighborhood's hot spot for trendy lattes, handcrafted pastries, and upscale baked eggs. I took Sarah's advice and opted for the brunch skillet overflowing with local Ali'i mushrooms. Each bite was exotic and creamy and would stick with me forever. To reinvent Morning Glass's fluffy skillet in my own kitchen, I swap in tender (more available) shiitakes and create a frittata for four, bubbling with gooey Italian cheese and swimming with earthy mushroom flavor.

In a large skillet, heat 1 tablespoon of the olive oil over medium heat. Add the sausage and brown it on all sides, 1 to 2 minutes per side. Remove the sausages from the pan, cut them crosswise into ¼-inch slices, and set aside.

In the same skillet the sausages were cooked in, heat the remaining 1 tablespoon olive oil. Add the mushrooms and cook until they are lightly browned, 2 to 3 minutes. Season them with a pinch each of salt and pepper.

Position a rack 4 to 6 inches from the heat and preheat the oven to broil.

In a bowl, whisk together the eggs, half-and-half, and remaining ½ teaspoon each salt and pepper.

In a large nonstick broilerproof skillet, melt the remaining 1½ tablespoons butter over medium heat. When the butter begins to foam and sizzle, pour the egg mixture into the pan. Evenly drop in the caramelized onions, chicken sausage, mushrooms, fontina, and thyme. Using a heatproof spatula, pull up the sides of the egg mixture and tilt the pan so the runny uncooked egg on the top goes to the bottom of the pan. Continue doing this until the frittata is mostly cooked through but still slightly liquid on top, 1 to 2 minutes, and then place the entire pan under the broiler.

Cook the frittata for 2 to 3 minutes, keeping the oven door slightly open and rotating the pan to get even heat if necessary. Keep a close eye, as the frittata can burn easily under the broiler.

The frittata is done when it's very fluffy and golden brown on top. Cut into wedges and serve.

Fanfare Tip

Instead of serving this brunch dish with traditional fruit or potatoes, go for a unique side salad instead. Bump up the sophistication with a mix of microgreens, dried cranberries, and toasted hazelnuts tossed in a light mustard vinaigrette.

Fig and Brie Frittata with Caramelized Leeks

This stunning masterpiece belongs in your belly, and maybe in the museum of natural *awesomeness*. (Don't burst my bubble—I'm certain that's a real place. It's where they keep Britney Spears and the original Nintendo.) Bright crimson figs and juicy caramelized leeks frolic through this fluffy frittata along with smooth, creamy Brie. Garnished with fresh mint and syrupy honey, your brunch guests just might linger to see what's on deck for dinner.

2½ tablespoons unsalted butter
1 leek, white and light green parts only, sliced
1 teaspoon honey
Kosher salt and coarse black pepper
6 large eggs
2 tablespoons half-and-half

4 large fresh figs, stemmed and cut into wedges
4 ounces Brie, cut into thin wedges

GARNISH
1 tablespoon chopped fresh mint
1 tablespoon honey

Position a rack 4 to 6 inches from the heat and preheat the oven to broil.

In a medium skillet, heat 1 tablespoon of the butter over low heat. Add the leek and honey, and cook the leeks, stirring occasionally, until golden and caramelized, 20 to 25 minutes. Season with a pinch each of salt and pepper.

In a medium nonstick broilerproof skillet, heat the remaining 1½ tablespoons butter over medium heat.

In a bowl, whisk the eggs with the half-and-half, ½ teaspoon salt, and ¼ teaspoon pepper. When the butter begins to foam and sizzle, pour the egg mixture into the pan and evenly drop in the caramelized leeks. Using a heatproof spatula, pull up the sides of the egg mix-

Fanfare Tip

Fresh figs are ideal for this dish, but if they're not in season, opt for another soft, juicy fruit like thinly sliced pear.

ture and tilt the pan so the runny uncooked egg on the top goes to the bottom of the pan. Continue doing this until the frittata is mostly cooked through but still slightly liquid on top, 1 to 2 minutes. The bottom should be lightly golden brown.

Scatter the figs and Brie slices on top and then place the entire pan under the broiler. Cook for 2 to 3 minutes, keeping the oven door slightly open and rotating the pan to get even heat if necessary. Keep a close eye, as the frittata can burn easily under the broiler.

The frittata is done when it's very fluffy and golden brown on top. Slide it out of the pan onto a cutting board and garnish with the fresh mint, drizzle with the honey, and cut into wedges.

Turkey Hash with Baked Runny Eggs

It's two days after Thanksgiving, and you've had more turkey sandwiches than you've seen in a year. Here's one more leftover-friendly recipe that travels your turkey to the breakfast table. This savory hash is topped with sharp cheddar and cracked eggs and finished in the oven for a yummy one-pan breakfast. During the eleven other months when your fridge isn't stocked with infinite Tupperware containers of turkey, opt for pulled rotisserie chicken instead.

½ pound small russet (baking) potatoes
1 tablespoon olive oil
½ tablespoon unsalted butter
¼ small sweet onion, roughly chopped
Kosher salt and coarse black pepper
½ cup shredded cooked turkey (or chicken)

1 medium clove garlic, minced
1 tablespoon chopped fresh sage
2 large eggs
1 tablespoon chopped fresh chives
¼ cup grated sharp white cheddar cheese

Position a rack about 6 inches from the top and preheat the oven to 400°F.

Grate the potatoes and place the shreds in cheesecloth or a kitchen towel. Squeeze out as much moisture as possible.

In an ovenproof medium skillet, heat the olive oil and butter over medium heat. Add the potatoes, onion, and ¼ teaspoon each salt and pepper and cook, stirring occasionally, until the potatoes are lightly golden, 5 to 7 minutes.

Add the turkey, garlic, and sage and toss to combine. Using a metal spatula, press the mixture down and form into a round pancake. Cook untouched until the bottom is golden brown, 3 to 5 minutes, then flip the pancake to cook the other side. If it comes apart, form it back together into its round shape. Cook until the second side is golden brown, about 3 more minutes.

When the hash is fully cooked and golden brown on both sides, create 2 wells and carefully crack 1 egg into each one. Sprinkle the chives and cheddar on top and season with salt and pepper.

Place the skillet in the oven and bake until the eggs are cooked to your liking, 4 to 6 minutes for runny yolks.

Fanfare Tip

For a Mexican spin on this dish, sauté your favorite variety of sliced bell or chili peppers along with the onions and sprinkle in some chili powder. Serve with diced avocado, fresh cilantro, and hot sauce.

Date with a Blueberry Muffin

Packed with protein-rich Greek yogurt and almond milk, these morning muffins are great for a quick, nutritious breakfast on the go. So moist and fluffy on the inside you'll be like, "No, I haven't seen the Muffin Man, and I really don't care."

2 cups rolled oats
2 teaspoons baking powder
½ teaspoon ground cinnamon
½ teaspoon kosher salt
½ cup packed dark brown sugar
½ cup blueberry Greek yogurt
½ cup vanilla almond milk

½ cup neutral oil (such as vegetable, grapeseed, or sunflower)
1 large egg, beaten
1 cup blueberries
½ cup chopped dates
2 tablespoons honey

Preheat the oven to 400°F. Grease a 12-cup muffin tin.

In a food processor, pulse 1½ cups of the rolled oats until very fine. Transfer to a large bowl and add the remaining ½ cup whole rolled oats, baking powder, cinnamon, salt, and brown sugar.

In a separate bowl, whisk together the Greek yogurt, almond milk, oil, and egg. A little at a time, mix the wet ingredients into the dry. Fold in the blueberries and chopped dates.

Divide the batter among the muffin cups and bake until the muffins are lightly golden and set, 18 to 20 minutes. When the muffins are cool enough to handle, remove them from the pan, arrange on a plate, and drizzle with the honey.

Fanfare Tips

- The dates in these muffins add an extra zing of sweetness without any additional refined sugar. Try substituting other dried fruits like cranberries, apricots, or figs.
- Are you a fan of the muffin top crunch? No, that's not an ab workout I just invented. I'm talking about that crisp sugary layer of awesome you sometimes find scattered along a pastry's surface. If you're down with the muffin crown, mix together 1 teaspoon cinnamon and 1 tablespoon granulated sugar and dust it over the muffins while they're still hot.

Open-Faced Scramble Sandwich with Roasted Tomato Butter

Sure, you flip fruit-studded pancakes or fancy omelets in your pajamas on a Saturday. But why can't *every* day begin with an extraordinary meal? I know those sunrise hours begin your busy day, but I have two words that will change your morning toast: compound butter. It's as simple as that. Butter—mixed with something else. Throw together this sweet roasted tomato butter the night before and slap it on your Monday morning egg sandwich for an epic start to your week.

6 large eggs
Kosher salt and freshly cracked black
    pepper
4 thick slices multigrain bread, toasted
1½ tablespoons unsalted butter

¼ cup grated parmesan cheese
Roasted Tomato Butter (recipe follows)
1 cup baby spinach
1 avocado, thinly sliced

Season the eggs with a pinch each of salt and cracked pepper and vigorously whisk until they are light and airy. Time placing your bread in the toaster so it will finish toasting at the same time your eggs are done.

In a medium nonstick skillet, heat the butter over medium-high heat. Once the butter begins to foam and sizzle, pour the eggs into the pan and scramble to your liking. Remove the eggs from the heat and immediately top with the parmesan.

Generously slather each slice of toast with Roasted Tomato Butter and top with a handful of spinach and the parmesan-covered eggs. Garnish with sliced avocado and season to taste with salt and cracked black pepper.

Fanfare Tip

Eating on the go? Slap another slice of bread on top for a mess-free, car-friendly meal. Dining at home? Substitute a fried egg for the scramble and poke the yolks just before serving.

Roasted Tomato Butter

MAKES ½ CUP

1½ cups sliced cherry tomatoes ★
1 tablespoon olive oil
1 teaspoon chopped fresh thyme
Kosher salt and coarse black pepper

3 tablespoons unsalted butter, at room
 temperature
½ teaspoon lemon juice

Preheat the oven to 400°F.

Spread the tomatoes on a baking sheet and toss with the olive oil, thyme, and ¼ teaspoon each salt and pepper. Roast until the tomatoes are wilted, 20 to 25 minutes.

In a small bowl, mash the roasted tomatoes with the softened butter and lemon juice. Season to taste with salt and pepper.

Cherry tomatoes had a starring role in the extraordinary breakfasts prepared by my mom. The smell of grainy, seeded wheat bread crisping in the toaster takes me back to her exquisite over-easy eggs (or what my family calls "sunny side down") that she would pair with fresh, acidic tomatoes. That fusion of crunchy toast, buttery yolks, and juicy bursts of sweetness are this recipe's inspiration.

Breakfast Quesadilla with Maple Sausage and Charred Poblanos

Burritos seem to have bullied quesadillas out of the running for Mexican-inspired breakfast foods. Well, not anymore, I say! Fold your favorite ingredients inside a flour tortilla for a scrambled spin on breakfast. Inside my quesadilla you'll find smoky, charred poblanos and creamy Monterey Jack cheese. For a double dose of heat, go for spicy sausage and jalapeños. For milder palates, opt for the sweet links instead.

2 poblano peppers (about 3 ounces each)
1 tablespoon olive oil
Kosher salt and coarse black pepper
4 fully cooked maple breakfast sausage
    links (about 1 ounce each)
6 large eggs
1½ tablespoons unsalted butter

2 burrito-size flour tortillas
1 cup packed baby spinach ★
1 cup shredded Monterey Jack cheese
2 tablespoons neutral oil (such as
    vegetable, grapeseed, or sunflower)
½ cup plain Greek yogurt or sour cream

Preheat the oven to 425°F.

On a baking sheet, drizzle the poblano peppers with the olive oil and season them with salt and pepper. Roast for 15 minutes, flipping them once halfway through so they are charred side up for the last half. When the peppers are cool enough to handle, slice off their tops, split them down the middle, scrape out the seeds, and roughly chop the flesh.

Reduce the oven temperature to 250°F.

In a small skillet, heat the sausages over medium heat until fully warmed through and lightly browned on all sides, 5 to 8 minutes. Roughly chop the sausages.

★ I remember my dad yanking tortillas and the contents of the vegetable drawer out of the fridge for quick-fix family dinners. My favorite filling was the leafy spinach, which would wilt into a tender layer between the golden brown exteriors of the quesadilla. This recipe keeps the spirit of the greens alive but transports the toasty triangles to the breakfast table.

In a bowl, season the eggs with a pinch each of salt and pepper and whisk until they are light and airy.

In a large nonstick skillet, heat the butter over medium-high heat. When the butter begins to foam and sizzle, pour in the eggs. As the outside begins to cook, lift up the eggs with a heatproof spatula so that the runny center flows to the sides of the pan. When the bottom is cooked—about 30 seconds—carefully flip the eggs so that they're now top-side down. If you're not comfortable flipping the eggs, scramble them with a spatula until they're soft and fluffy, 15 to 20 seconds after the bottom is cooked. Immediately remove the eggs from the heat and split them down the middle so you have two half-moons.

On one half of each tortilla, layer the poblanos, eggs, sausage, spinach, and Monterey Jack cheese, and sprinkle with salt and pepper. Fold the tortillas over to make a quesadilla shape.

In a large skillet, heat 1 tablespoon of the neutral oil over medium heat. Add one quesadilla and cook until golden brown and crispy, 2 to 3 minutes per side. Place it on a baking sheet to keep warm in the oven. Prepare the second quesadilla with the remaining ingredients.

When both quesadillas have been cooked, slice them into triangles and serve with the Greek yogurt or sour cream.

Fanfare Tip

Make breakfast quesadillas a weekend tradition, and design inspired creations with a different weekly theme. For a Greek twist, add feta and roasted red peppers. For an Italian spin, use fresh basil, roasted tomatoes, and Pecorino Romano.

Holy Bagel

The little round hole omitted from the bagel's center is a metaphor for the missing piece in my heart . . .

. . . that fell out as a child when I realized you can get good bagels only in the Northeast.

It's 1989, and we're packing our things to depart from Pennsylvania. I bid farewell to the familiar pieces of my surroundings. Goodbye deli-sliced pastrami. Goodbye authentic Jewish rye bread. Goodbye oniony bagels. Granted, I was certain this was merely a temporary separation because I would find alternative delis and bagel shops in our new town of Raleigh, North Carolina. Yes, these were the very thoughts of my almost four-year-old self.

I was a very wistful child.

The following weeks we settled happily into our Southern environment, but something felt strange. Sunday mornings weren't the same. Sure, there were substitute bagels, but they were dull and pasty. One weekend we flew to New Jersey to visit my grandparents, and I clung to my grandfather's leg silently singing songs of smoked salmon.

I awoke the next morning to the gurgling of the coffeepot and the earthy, smoky aroma of dark French roast. And then I heard it . . . a crinkle that could have come only from the brown paper bag of a Jewish deli. I rocketed toward the kitchen, where I was greeted with a spread fit to feed the whole town. This abundant buffet boasted white plastic cups of veggie cream cheese dotted with peppers and scallions, stacks of parchment paper concealing paper-thin slices of smoky Nova and salty whitefish, and baskets chock-full of still-warm, glistening bagels in every flavor. The real deal.

These Northern-bred, plump, yeasty bagels with their crisp golden brown skin and tender, fluffy insides were as fantastically wonderful and unique as the

Someone pass me the capers.

family I enjoyed them with. We all had our own bagel-centric quirks. My mom favored fresh, juicy tomato slices and the thinnest Swiss to top her meaty mountain of glistening Nova, whitefish and Greek olives on the side. For me, it was abundant dollops of whipped cream cheese whose silkiness sent me over the moon. And for my grandma, the perfectly petite mini bagels that barely covered her plate but filled her heart with joy. I had always had an appreciation for this lavish feast, but realizing that we no longer lived a caper's throw from these spectacularly authentic bagels made me treasure it that much more.

★ **Smoked Salmon Benedict with Everything Hollandaise** (page 38): For my Smoked Salmon Benedict I call upon crispy English muffins—always available, delicious, and easy to find—in place of perfectly toasted bagels. I've turned the "everything" part of this traditional dish into an oniony, buttery sauce that trickles over delicately poached eggs.

Smoked Salmon Benedict with Everything Hollandaise

I know there are poppy seeds stuck in my teeth. And I don't care. If you feel the same way I do, then this breakfast has your name all over it. This luxurious dish unites creamy eggs Benedict with an equally popular morning classic: everything bagels with smoked salmon. In this fusion of two favorites, toasted English muffins are topped with a light spread of cream cheese, salty smoked salmon, drippy poached eggs, rich hollandaise permeated with garlic and onion, and a crowning of crunchy sesame seeds, poppy seeds, and coarse crystals of salt. I know. I'm as excited as you are.

EVERYTHING HOLLANDAISE

2 large egg yolks

1½ tablespoons lemon juice

½ teaspoon onion powder

¼ teaspoon grated garlic

4 tablespoons (½ stick) unsalted butter, melted

Pinch of kosher salt

Pinch of cayenne pepper

½ teaspoon poppy seeds

½ teaspoon white sesame seeds

½ teaspoon black sesame seeds

½ teaspoon very coarse, large-grained salt (like you would find on an everything bagel)

BENEDICT

2 tablespoons distilled white vinegar

8 large eggs

4 English muffins, split

8 tablespoons whipped cream cheese

8 ounces smoked salmon

2 medium vine-ripened or Roma (plum) tomatoes, sliced into ¼-inch-thick rounds

Kosher salt and coarse black pepper

Make the Everything Hollandaise: In a small saucepan, vigorously whisk the egg yolks, lemon juice, onion powder, and garlic over low heat. Whisk until the mixture has doubled in size, and then, still whisking, slowly drizzle in the melted butter about a tablespoon at a time. Season with the salt and cayenne, then remove from the heat and set the hollandaise aside.

In a small bowl, mix together the poppy seeds, white sesame seeds, black sesame seeds, and large-grained salt. Set the "everything" mixture aside.

Prepare the Benedict: Fill a large bowl with cold water and set it beside the stove. Fill a sauté pan or a deep, high-sided skillet halfway with water and bring to a boil over medium-high heat. Once the water begins to boil, add the vinegar and reduce the heat to a simmer so there are almost no bubbles.

Crack one of the eggs into a ramekin or custard cup and gently slide the egg into the simmering water. Repeat with the next 3 eggs so your first batch is 4 eggs total. Cook the eggs for 3 minutes, remove them with a slotted spoon, and place them in the bowl of cold water. Repeat with the remaining 4 eggs, and then turn the heat under the poaching water down to low.

At this point, place the English muffins in the toaster and toast until golden brown.

Return the hollandaise to low heat and whisk to reincorporate the ingredients and gently reheat the mixture, about 1 minute.

Spread each toasted English muffin half with whipped cream cheese and top with smoked salmon, tomato slices, and a pinch of salt and pepper. Return the poached eggs to the warm water to reheat, about 1 minute, and then one at a time dab them just before serving on a clean kitchen towel to drain any excess water. Top each tomato with a poached egg, a spoonful of the hollandaise, and a sprinkle of the "everything" mixture.

Fanfare Tip

Try whisking different flavors into your hollandaise for unique variations on this buttery sauce. For a spicy kick, add in several additional pinches of cayenne and a few drops of hot sauce. For a touch of sweetness, stir in some maple syrup and orange zest.

The Museum of Breakfast

I will never forget the evening my mom led me into her closet and pulled an aged scrapbook from behind a mountain of shoeboxes. I was certain she was about to reveal my *actual* baby photos along with an enchanted story of how I was born with a tail. She hugged the worn book to her heart and began to speak with a surreal gaze over my shoulder, as if the past were coming to life right behind me. She then shared her cherished childhood memories of Tripp Lake Camp in Maine, her beloved summertime utopia, where everything, especially the French toast, was legendary. She trailed on about this rich breakfast delicacy—an ethereal buttery goodness drenched in maple syrup—evoking it so vividly that it began to thunder.

Well, inside my stomach.

Once upon a camp cafeteria, my fifteen-year-old mom remained by herself at an empty table, refusing to leave. It was her very last morning of her very last summer at Tripp Lake, and a miracle had occurred. Of all the breakfast dishes that might have been served, it was the luscious French toast that appeared: thick, crispy, gloriously deep-fried, golden brown triangles exploding with egg and cinnamon. She sat, oblivious to all else, letting each bite melt into her mouth for the final time. On a whim, she tucked a still-warm piece of the toast inside her napkin, and flew home with it carefully stashed inside her suitcase, eventually rewrapping it with plastic to keep it safe for eternity.

Time-traveling in a vortex of memories, I suddenly realized we were back in the closet. A childlike grin stretched across my mom's face and it was as if the magnificent breakfast—maple-infused and flecked with gold—were once again right under her nose.

And then all of a sudden, it was.

Sandwiched between the pages of the faded album was the mythic French toast from her last summer at camp—oh, and several blond locks she snipped from Chandler—her dreamy counselor crush. *What, like you've never done anything weird?* As for the toast, it has almost reached its fiftieth birthday and most likely will outlive us all. While some may find it odd that my parents' home is technically a museum for the world's oldest breakfast article, I am thankful for my mom and her determination to preserve what was a divinely delicious experience. Not to mention Chandler's stray hairs (although I do wish we

Mom, circa 1978, returning to the home of her beloved French toast.

had planted them in the backyard to sprout a tree of babelicious eighteen-year-old boys). When I think of my mom's passion for prolonging the life of this food memory, I realize it's as if her childhood self was laying the foundation for what would eventually become the heart and soul of her daughter's life work. Don't you love when things come full circle?

★ **Banana Bacon Bread Pudding with Cinnamon Rum Sauce** (page 42): To bring this masterpiece back to life in the modern world, I bathe day-old bread cubes in a light custard—perfumed with vanilla and nutmeg—and toss them with creamy bananas and crispy bacon. In place of traditional syrup, I drizzle on a rich, gooey cinnamon sauce spiked with dark caramel-scented rum. (Please feel free to prepare this bread pudding and keep it inside this cookbook to show your children someday. Or maybe just snap a photo. To each his own.)

Banana Bacon Bread Pudding with Cinnamon Rum Sauce

Hats off to the first person who dumped their entire breakfast into one pan and thought, "Now, I shall stick this in the oven." For those of us who prefer a little savory with our sweet, this brunch-friendly bread pudding blends salty, crisp bacon with tender bananas and chewy raisins. For those of us who enjoy a Sunday morning buzz, cinnamon rum sauce does the trick.

2½ cups cubed (1-inch) day-old country-style bread
6 slices bacon, cooked and roughly chopped
2 very ripe bananas, roughly chopped
2 tablespoons raisins
2 large eggs

½ cup whole or 2% milk
¼ cup packed light brown sugar
1 teaspoon pure vanilla extract
⅛ teaspoon grated nutmeg
Pinch of kosher salt
Cinnamon Rum Sauce (recipe follows)

Preheat the oven to 350°F. Grease a 7 x 11-inch baking dish.

Layer the bread cubes, bacon, bananas, and raisins in the baking dish. In a large bowl, whisk together the eggs, milk, brown sugar, vanilla, nutmeg, and salt. Pour the egg mixture into the baking dish and toss to combine. Press down to make sure that all of the bread is evenly saturated.

Bake until the custard is set and a knife slides out clean, 45 to 50 minutes. While the bread pudding is still hot, pour the rum sauce over top. Divide into even portions and serve.

Cinnamon Rum Sauce

MAKES ¼ CUP

1 tablespoon unsalted butter
2 tablespoons half-and-half
1 tablespoon brown sugar

1½ tablespoons dark rum
¼ teaspoon ground cinnamon
Pinch of kosher salt

In a small saucepan, whisk together the butter, half-and-half, brown sugar, rum, cinnamon, and salt over low heat. Once the mixture is thoroughly combined, increase the heat to medium-low. Simmer, whisking frequently, until thickened and glossy, 5 to 7 minutes.

Fanfare Tip

For tasty twists on this decadent sauce, swap out the rum for whiskey, the brown sugar for maple syrup, or the cinnamon for coconut extract.

Chapter 2

Soups and FANwiches

As a kid I would have handed over every cent of my milk money in order to hold on to my bologna and cheese on white. Today, my between-bread behaviors have become more refined. This chapter spotlights sophisticated soups and sandwiches with an artful twist.

The FAN Club with Roasted Eggplant and Pickled Red Onions

Groucho Marx once said, "I wouldn't want to belong to any club that would have me as a member." Well, Mr. Marx, you would have been invited to *my club* anytime. Sandwich, that is. In this meat-free twist on the traditional triple-decker, I've ditched the third layer of bread to make room for an abundance of tasty veg-friendly fillings. Hearty roasted eggplant meets creamy dill sauce meets sweet pickled onions.

All for one, and avocado for all.

Or something like that.

½ cup water
½ cup white wine vinegar
1 tablespoon sugar
Kosher salt and coarse black pepper
1 small red onion, thinly sliced
½ cup olive oil
2 teaspoons dried oregano

1 large eggplant (about 1½ pounds), peeled and cut crosswise into ½-inch-thick rounds
1 avocado
Creamy Dill Sauce (recipe follows)
8 slices pumpernickel bread
2 cups baby spinach leaves

In a small saucepan, whisk together the water, vinegar, sugar, and 1 teaspoon salt over high heat.

Place the sliced red onion in an airtight heatproof container. Once the vinegar mixture reaches a boil, pour it over the onion and cover the container. Let the onion sit at room temperature for 30 minutes.

Preheat the oven to 400°F.

In a small bowl, whisk together the oil and dried oregano. Brush the herb oil on both sides of the eggplant and season with salt and pepper. Arrange the eggplant rounds on a baking sheet and roast until tender, flipping halfway through cooking, 16 to 18 minutes.

In a bowl, mash the avocado with a pinch of salt. Spread dill sauce on each slice of pumpernickel. Top 4 of the slices with the avocado mash, spinach, eggplant rounds, and a generous pinch of pickled onions (you'll have more onions than you need here, but check out the Flippidy-Doo, on opposite page). Top each sandwich with the other slice of pumpernickel and cut on the diagonal.

Creamy Dill Sauce

MAKES ⅓ CUP

3 tablespoons plain Greek yogurt
2 tablespoons mayonnaise
1 teaspoon Dijon mustard

1 tablespoon chopped fresh dill
1 tablespoon fresh lemon juice
Kosher salt and coarse black pepper

In a small bowl, whisk together the yogurt, mayonnaise, mustard, dill, and lemon juice. Season to taste with salt and pepper.

Flippidy-Doo

Make the full amount of pickled onions for this recipe. You will likely have a bit more than you need for 4 sandwiches, so here are three additional recipes from this book where these sweet, vinegary onions can find a cozy home:

- Pulled Buffalo Chicken Tacos with Red Onions and Poblanos (page 122)
- Open-Faced Scramble Sandwich with Roasted Tomato Butter (page 32)
- Vegetarian Lettuce Wraps with Sweet and Sour Tomato Vinaigrette (page 94)

The Forest of Sandwiches

Many moons ago, my best friend, John, and I braved a magical forest full of elves for two club sandwiches.

Okay, so there weren't any elves. And there were no mystical fairies or gnarled trees that offered us three wishes, but we did trot miles through some scary woods one summer in pursuit of a snack. As an adolescent in a suburban neighborhood, if your parents aren't able to drive you somewhere, you have two options: wait until they get home or distract yourself by building a fort. John and I chose nonexistent option number three: walk until you reach a destination that has ham and turkey.

Me and my childhood partner in crime, John. And by crime, I mean sandwiches and singing. This is John and me at our first, and surprisingly last, band gig.

After what felt like hours of flinging aside spiderwebs, belting *"Baby One More Time,"* and blaming the other for farting—we arrived at our submarine finish line: Jersey Mike's. Dripping with herby oils and slathered in creamy mayo, the luscious sandwiches we lusted after were an unforgettable, much-deserved treat. I can still taste the sweet tang of the paper-thin onions doused in sharp red vinegar.

John was my very best friend, my partner in amateur crime—like driving my mom's car around our circular driveway once when we were thirteen—and the only other member of my band. (Years later, John would go on to be the musical director of a professional a cappella group and audition for *American Idol*, yet in our rock duo, he let me be the star.) Together we created a cooking show for which we once prepared my parents' famous brownies (see "The Brownie Legacy," page 207). But mostly we just snacked on chocolate chips and talked to the camera about our aprons. We were fourteen. John appreciated the elegant herbs in my dad's chicken and the artisanal cheese my mom crumbled into our salads. But especially, he shared my extreme enthusiasm for a sensational sandwich.

As I grew up and became a scratch-made sandwich enthusiast, I began to reimagine that memorable lunch that had once lured me through the woods. Mayo no longer made an appearance as I discovered that I could whisk up a creamy dressing of my own in no time. I replaced thinly sliced meat with herby roasted eggplant and plunked delicate onion rounds directly into vinegar. I'll have to consult with John, but I'd like to think my reinvention is a sandwich worth walking for.

★ **The FAN Club with Roasted Eggplant and Pickled Red Onions** (page 46): Toodles turkey. I've vegged out this sandwich with oregano-dusted eggplant, mashed avocado, and crunchy spinach.

Grilled Eggplant Banh Mi

Smoky grilled eggplant meets crisp veggies and a citrusy smear of lime cream for a meat-free alternative to this traditional Vietnamese pork sandwich. Sweet rosemary and black pepper peanuts add a unique, unexpected crunch.

Where's the beef? You won't care.

2 carrots, peeled into ribbons
¼ cup distilled white vinegar
¼ cup sugar
Kosher salt and coarse black pepper
⅓ cup olive oil
1 teaspoon ground cumin
1 medium eggplant (about 1 pound), unpeeled and sliced lengthwise into ½-inch-thick slabs
¼ cup plain Greek yogurt
1 tablespoon fresh lime juice

1 teaspoon honey
1 thick 28-inch baguette, cut crosswise into 4 even pieces and split open
4 Persian cucumbers, unpeeled and thinly sliced on the diagonal
¼ cup roughly chopped fresh cilantro
1 small jalapeño, seeded and thinly sliced
½ cup roughly chopped Honey-Roasted Rosemary and Black Pepper Peanuts (page 108)

Place the carrots in an airtight container. Whisk together the vinegar, sugar, and a pinch of salt and pour the mixture over the carrots. Cover the container and let sit at room temperature for 20 minutes.

Preheat a grill or grill pan to medium-high.

In a small bowl, whisk together the olive oil and cumin. Brush the cumin oil on both sides of the eggplant and season with salt and pepper. Grill the eggplant slabs until tender and lightly charred, 2 to 3 minutes per side.

In a small bowl, whisk together the yogurt, lime juice, and honey. Season the lime cream to taste with salt and pepper.

To assemble the sandwiches, spread all 8 baguette slices with lime cream and top 4 with even portions of the grilled eggplant, cucumbers, pickled carrots, cilantro, jalapeños, and chopped peanuts. Top with the remaining baguette slices and cut each sandwich in half on a diagonal.

Fanfare Tip

Swirl some Sriracha into your lime cream for a sandwich that packs a punch. To double the heat, leave the jalapeño seeds in.

Toasted Elvis PBB&J

Peanut butter and banana is the new pink—and Elvis would agree. Riffing off my own child-hood classics is my game, but this one goes out to the King. Twist the lid back on that jelly jar, because the J in this FANwich requires you to get fresh with some raspberries. This combo of jammy, tart mashed fruit, sweet sliced bananas, and crunchy toasted sunflower seeds will have you *all shook up.*

2 tablespoons unsalted raw sunflower
    seeds
½ cup raspberries
1 tablespoon sugar
Pinch of kosher salt

8 slices multigrain bread, toasted
½ cup creamy peanut butter ★
2 ripe bananas, sliced into ½-inch-thick
    rounds
2 tablespoons honey

In a dry small skillet, toast the sunflower seeds over medium-low heat, tossing frequently, until lightly golden and very fragrant, about 5 minutes. Immediately remove the seeds from the pan and transfer to a bowl to stop the cooking process.

In a small saucepan, mash the raspberries, sugar, and salt. Simmer over medium-high heat, stirring frequently, until the raspberries are broken down and have a thick jamlike consistency, 3 to 4 minutes.

Spread all 8 slices of toast evenly with the peanut butter.

Top 4 of the slices with bananas, raspberry mash, sunflower seeds, and a drizzle of honey. Top each sandwich with the other piece of peanut butter toast and slice on the diagonal.

Fanfare Tip

Kick up the Elvis with a few slices of crispy bacon. Any nut allergies in the family? Swap out the peanut butter for sunflower seed butter.

★ I was certain Elvis and I would get married. Or at least co-headline a tour. My obsession with the King sprouted when I watched a documentary on his life and discovered his love for the combination of peanut butter and bananas. Clearly we were soul mates as I, too, adored the creamy, comforting spread and paired it often with the sweet yellow fruit. The tragic story of his death (news to me) concluded the biography and put an abrupt halt to my matrimonial musical. I was devastated, alone, confused . . . and hungry. At least I still had my peanut butter.

The Chicken Salad Chronicles

Typically when you quit a job, proper etiquette is to not return.

The following story proves that theory wrong. It is also the tale of a life-changing chicken salad sandwich. If you're from the North Raleigh area, you grew up on Boondini's. This unassuming self-dubbed "sandwich superstore" thrives on devoted customers who rely on their faithful favorites to carry them through the day. I spent years navigating my way through the comforting home-style menu, never quite settling on *my* personal favorite.

And then one day, everything changed.

It was May 2008, and I was home from college in search of a job. I had wandered into Boondini's with my heart (hangover) set on a gooey griddled pimento cheese melt. A sign marked "Part-time Help Wanted" hung on the door. Within days I was behind the counter portioning out herby homemade dressings and whisking sugar with fresh, citrusy juice for glorious orangeade.

Demonstrating my love for Boondini's after a euphoric chicken salad sandwich experience.

Inspired to sample something new, one day I went home with chicken salad on toasted sunflower bread. I perched on my parents' couch and shed the sandwich's foil wrapping. The golden seeded bread was overflowing with iceberg shreds and an oversize dollop of the juiciest, creamiest chicken salad I had ever seen. My first bite was an eruption of savory flavors—luscious, garlicky, herbaceous—all working together in one magnificent mouthful. In that moment, I had found "the one," and I knew we were going to be together forever.

Not two weeks later, I was offered a unique opportunity at a restaurant where I had recently interned. I handed in my orangeade spoon and said good-bye to Boondini's. I was ashamed of my short-lived employment and walked out fearing my relationship with the chicken salad on sunflower bread had come to a close. To my surprise, I found myself back in line several days later—and then several days again after that. This ritual lunch became so frequent that even after I moved to California, Boondini's employees saw me so often during my visits home that they had no idea I had ever left the state. As most of my stories do, this anecdote begins with a meal and ends with a moral. Overcome with the embarrassment of quitting, what had convinced me to return?

I realized that as an adult, you must confidently display your maturity. You must face your fears and recognize when it's appropriate to hold your head high.

And most important, you must never, *ever* let anything stand in the way of a good chicken salad sandwich.

★ **Creamy Pulled Chicken Salad and Bacon Wraps** (page 54): For my spin on chicken salad, I've added grassy dill and freshened up the base with citrus and tangy yogurt. Salty bacon adds crunch to this delicate wrap.

Creamy Pulled Chicken Salad and Bacon Wraps

Step aside average chicken salad sandwich. This is the big leagues, and we're bringing home the bacon. Flavorful shreds of roasted rotisserie chicken mingle with tangy notes of dill and oniony scallions in this light, yogurt-dressed lunch staple.

8 slices thick-cut hickory bacon

CHICKEN SALAD

1 rotisserie chicken (about 2 pounds), meat pulled (2 to 3 cups)
1 cup chopped celery with leafy tops
¼ cup chopped dill pickles
2 tablespoons chopped fresh dill
½ cup chopped scallions, white and light green parts only
¾ cup plain Greek yogurt
¼ cup mayonnaise
1 tablespoon Dijon mustard

2 tablespoons pickle juice or white wine vinegar
Juice of 1 lemon
1 tablespoon honey
Kosher salt and coarse black pepper

WRAPS

8 whole wheat tortillas (10 inches)
8 large green leaf lettuce or romaine leaves
4 vine-ripened tomatoes, sliced into ¼-inch-thick rounds
Kosher salt and coarse black pepper

Preheat the oven to 400°F.

Place the bacon slices on a wire rack set inside a rimmed baking sheet. Bake until crispy, 18 to 20 minutes. When the bacon is cooked, set it aside on paper towels to drain any excess grease.

Fanfare Tip

Going light on the carbs this season? Drop the wrap altogether and dollop big portions of chicken salad and bacon inside the lettuce leaves for a high-protein picnic lunch or a refreshing midday snack.

Make the chicken salad: In a large bowl, combine the shredded chicken, celery, pickles, dill, and scallions.

In a small bowl, whisk together the yogurt, mayo, mustard, pickle juice, lemon juice, and honey. Season to taste with salt and pepper. Several tablespoons at a time, pour the dressing over the chicken mixture, tossing to combine, until the chicken salad is coated to your liking. Taste and add salt and pepper if needed.

Assemble the wraps: Top each tortilla with a lettuce leaf, 1 slice of bacon, a heaping scoop of chicken salad, and tomatoes. Season the tomatoes with salt and pepper, roll the wrap burrito-style, tucking in the ends, and halve on the diagonal.

My Bologna Has a First Name

Remember the good old days when you'd flick the string off a slice of bologna, bite out three holes, and wear it as a mask?

Me, too.

Prosciutto is the elegant, three-times-removed, most distant cousin of bologna. Just being near it makes you feel classy. One tender, translucent taste of prosciutto across your tongue, and you're swirling a Sauvignon Blanc in a stemless wineglass and saying things like, "Is this *local* radicchio?"

I adore prosciutto, not just for its soft buttery flavor, but for the nostalgia that it feeds me. There is a story from my childhood that my mom loves to share. It is not a chronicle from the Fanny Slater roster of academic achievements, as my most dignified scholastic honor was receiving the "Best Rester Award" in kindergarten. It is not the anecdote of the crushed-velvet-clad, Gloria Estefan—belting, all-girl musical ensemble I was in, although my mom is quite proud of that, too. The tale my mom eagerly narrates is a saga similar to *Goldilocks and the Three Bears*. Except that instead of an intrusive blonde, there is a sassy young tomboy who occasionally skateboarded, and instead of three bears . . . there is a package of bologna.

As the story goes, nearly every afternoon my childhood self would nimbly re-

While many children my age enjoyed a slice of bologna on white, I preferred it in the form of a frightening yet edible face mask.

peat the following activities. First, I would comb the fridge in search of my favorite snack, bologna. Scanning the kitchen to make sure I was alone, I would gently wriggle out a pink disk, carefully peel the thin casing away from its outer surface . . . and then fling the glossy skin-like string across the room with the jubilation of a choir singer bursting into a ballad. I would then nibble out three very deliberate holes and place the shiny meat mask onto my face. Oscar Mayer and I would prance through the house to impress the nearest family member or cat. After everyone was thoroughly entertained, I would continue on my journey of meat and mayhem—obliviously smearing every doorknob, windowpane, furnishing, and fixture in the house with a glistening coat of grease. Hygiene and I would not be acquainted for another three years, when I discovered boys and in third grade got engaged to Matt Petrovick, who gave me what I'm still convinced was a real diamond ring.

Despite having to follow me around with a roll of paper towels, my mom thought I was the silliest being ever to land on earth, and my dad and sister agreed. The cats also benefited terrifically from my attachment to lunchmeat, so it was a win-win for all. As for me, it was as if—on a deeper level—life was already propelling me to spread my culinary enthusiasm anywhere I could make my mark. As if my five-year-old self somehow already knew that my future calling was to be one with food.

The moral of the story: Playing with your food can have lifelong benefits, and that's no baloney. Today, I opt for the elegance of prosciutto—but I wear it only on the weekends.

★ **Parmesan-Crusted Prosciutto and White Cheddar Wraps** (page 58): I marry the marvelous cured meat with sharp cheddar in a wrapped-up, light, and luscious improv on my old childhood standby, bologna and cheese. No cleanup required, as it will easily disappear without a trace.

Parmesan-Crusted Prosciutto and White Cheddar Wraps

This is not your typical ham and cheese sandwich. Sharp, tangy cheddar meets delicate, earthy prosciutto and sweet basil in this melty wrap that will awaken your taste buds and raise your lunch IQ. Lightly showered in honey and encrusted with parmesan, this sweet and salty FANwich is meant to be savored slowly.

2 whole wheat tortillas (8 inches)
½ cup shredded sharp white cheddar
   cheese
6 thin slices prosciutto
6 large basil leaves
1 small vine-ripened or Roma tomato,
   sliced into ¼-inch-thick rounds

Kosher salt and cracked black pepper
2 tablespoons unsalted butter
¼ cup grated parmesan
2 teaspoons honey

Fill the tortillas with even portions of the cheddar, prosciutto, basil, and tomatoes. Season with salt and pepper and tightly roll the wrap closed, leaving the ends open and untucked.

In a medium nonstick skillet, heat 1 tablespoon of the butter over medium heat. Brush a small amount of the melted butter from the pan onto one side of the wraps, sprinkle with half of the parmesan, and press down so it sticks. Place the wraps parmesan-side down in the pan and cook until the parmesan is crusted and golden brown, 2 to 3 minutes.

Repeat the butter and parmesan process on the other side of the wraps and flip them over to cook until golden, about 2 more minutes.

Halve the wraps on the diagonal and evenly drizzle with the honey.

Fanfare Tip

Not a meat eater but still craving the gooey goodness of this wrap? Substitute thinly sliced pears instead of the prosciutto for a vegetarian's dream come true.

Turkey and Balsamic Fig Jam Wraps with Orange Goat Cheese Spread

We live in a world of turkey and mayo, but should *dream* in a place where turkey meets balsamic fig jam and tangy goat cheese spread. This recipe makes all your dreams come true by transforming an average lunchtime wrap into an unexpected eruption of sweet and savory. Pillow not included.

½ cup Balsamic Fig Jam (page 220)
2 tablespoons whipped cream cheese, at room temperature
4 ounces goat cheese, at room temperature
¼ teaspoon grated orange zest
2 tablespoons fresh orange juice
1 tablespoon honey

Pinch of kosher salt
6 honey wheat or whole wheat tortillas (8 inches)
1 pound thinly sliced roast turkey
1 tart apple, such as Granny Smith, thinly sliced
2 cups baby arugula

Make the balsamic fig jam and set it aside to come to room temperature.

In a small bowl, whisk together the cream cheese, goat cheese, orange zest, orange juice, honey, and salt.

Lay the tortillas out flat and spread with the orange goat cheese mixture and balsamic fig jam. Top each tortilla with even portions of the turkey, apples, and arugula. Tightly roll each wrap closed, leaving the ends open and untucked, and halve on the diagonal.

Fanfare Tip

For a melty version of this wrap, trade the goat cheese spread for Brie and pull out the panini press.

Boozy Fig Chili with Cinnamon and Orange

SERVES 4 TO 6 (7½ CUPS)

Figs and chili? Have I lost my marbles? Why, I believe I've just found them. There is nothing predictable about this cinnamon-dusted chili. Permeated with the sweet essence of figs and the pungent malty bite of an amber ale, this is a soup to savor. I suggest pairing it with something salty to offset the warm flavors—so fasten your garlic bread and let's get started.

2 tablespoons olive oil
1 pound ground turkey
Kosher salt and coarse black pepper
1 tablespoon unsalted butter
1 medium shallot, minced
2 poblano peppers, seeded and diced
½ pound dried figs, stemmed and chopped
1 tablespoon tomato paste
1 bottle (12 ounces) amber or red ale (see Fanfare Tips)

3 cups lower-sodium vegetable stock
1 can (28 ounces) diced tomatoes
1 can (15 ounces) black beans, drained and rinsed
2 teaspoons chili powder
2 teaspoons ground cumin
2 teaspoons paprika
2 teaspoons dried oregano
½ teaspoon ground cinnamon
2 teaspoons honey
1 teaspoon grated orange zest ★

In a large pot, heat the oil over medium heat. Add the ground turkey, ½ teaspoon salt, and ¼ teaspoon pepper and brown until the meat is evenly cooked, about 5 minutes. Remove the meat with a slotted spoon and set it aside.

Many aromatic soups simmered on the stove of my childhood. The secret ingredient that lingered below the surface? Orange zest. This bright floral note inspires my chili today, as I *always* crave a hint of citrus with my savory.

Melt the butter in the pot. Add the shallot, poblanos, and figs and cook until the shallots are translucent, 3 to 5 minutes. Add the tomato paste, whisk to break it up, and cook for 1 minute. Add the meat back to the pot, pour in the beer, and scrape up any browned bits from the bottom. Add the vegetable stock, tomatoes, beans, chili powder, cumin, paprika, oregano, cinnamon, and honey and bring to a boil.

Reduce the heat to low and simmer uncovered, stirring occasionally, for 1 hour. Taste for salt and adjust the seasoning. Just before serving, stir in the orange zest.

Fanfare Tips

- Finish this chili with a hefty handful of shredded parmesan and a side of buttery garlic bread for a sharp, savory burst of flavor to balance the sweetness from the figs and orange zest.
- Choose a beer with a fruity, caramel-like flavor and a fresh, balanced hoppiness. If the beer you end up using is exceptionally hoppy, add more honey to taste to balance out the bitterness.

I'm a Slave 4 Gazpacho

One summer, our orange Persian cat Lieutenant Mango developed a habit of peeing everywhere but his litter box. I hired myself as his full-time parole officer. Apparently this wasn't what my dad had meant by "get a job."

My parents had grown tired of financially supporting my Britney Spears CD collection, and my dreams of making it big as a ventriloquist were shattered when I realized that dolls in suits are haunted. So out into the real world I went in pursuit of stable employment. Being around food was a must, and I assumed that Quiznos wouldn't hire me back after a squabble we'd had the previous summer. Just my luck, a small grocery store opened nearby and was looking for help in the prepared foods department. The robust, middle-aged apron-clad woman looked me up and down. She had celery in her hair. Barely weighing in at 100 pounds, sporting dirty blonde highlights and several ear piercings, I stared directly into her glare and cleared my throat. "I, um, know how to use a knife," I said boldly, but quietly.

"You're hired."

I was handed a sharp blade with a blue handle and a pile of colorful veggies. I began chopping. I glanced up as customers drifted by and placed plastic containers packed to the brim with tuna salad into their carts. I realized that the fennel bouncing around under my knife would soon be a small piece of someone's lunch. I was nervous and excited all at once—pretty much the same feeling as peeling the wrapper off my newest Britney album.

Each week, I was entrusted with additional tasks. I seasoned the split pea soup with salt. I whisked vinaigrettes. I plucked dozens of rotisserie chickens. One day I was handed several pages of recipes. Up until this point I'd been given direct instruction from the chef, who would peer over my shoulder to make sure I didn't forget the pimentos in the pimento cheese. I spun around, but found myself alone in the prep kitchen. I had been given full responsibility. No one was telling me how

Age sixteen. My very first job, as a sandwich artist at Quiznos. I took a bit of poetic license by adding lettuce to the Black Angus sub. I was fired. It would not be the last time.

many scallions to chop or where to place the grapes. I looked down at my first solo task: gazpacho. I scanned the ingredients.

"Someone spelled 'salsa' wrong," I whispered to myself.

Suddenly, small squares of multicolored peppers soared through the air, and I realized I had lost myself in a trance of dicing. I gazed into the crimson-filled chrome bowl and sampled my creation. It was crisp, acidic, savory, and light all at once. This bite, and the freedom I was given that day to explore my skills in the kitchen, would forever inspire my future homemade soups. I'm constantly curious to experiment with parallel flavors as well as opposing textures. Instead of a sharp red onion, I prefer the sweet gentle sting of a shallot. Instead of creamy or crunchy, I like to pair them together in one bite. That's the fun in cooking. Even if someone hands you a recipe, you let your palate lead the path.

Unless you work at Quiznos. Then you probably want to do what they tell you.

★ **Avocado and Heirloom Tomato Gazpacho** (page 64): I've taken a nontraditional trail by blending the base of the soup, but reserving some of the finely chopped veggies for a crisp, fresh garnish. I've also swapped in luscious, multicolored heirloom tomatoes for a rich, succulent, homegrown tomato tang.

Avocado and Heirloom Tomato Gazpacho

Gazpacho is like salsa's big sister (many of the ingredients are the same), but "gazpacho" is much more fun to say. For a twist on textures, I leave a small portion of the soup in chunky, diced pieces and blend the rest with creamy avocado until velvety smooth.

1 yellow bell pepper, diced (about 1 cup)

1 orange bell pepper, diced (about 1 cup)

1 large seedless cucumber, peeled and diced (about 1¼ cups)

1 medium shallot, minced

1 medium clove garlic, minced

2 medium heirloom tomatoes, diced (about 1 cup)

¼ cup chopped fresh flat-leaf parsley

Juice of 1 lime

1 tablespoon Louisiana-style hot sauce, such as Texas Pete

2 tablespoons champagne vinegar or red wine vinegar

¼ cup olive oil

Kosher salt and coarse black pepper

1 avocado, roughly chopped

½ cup plain Greek yogurt, for garnish

In a large bowl, combine the bell peppers, cucumber, shallot, garlic, tomatoes, parsley, lime juice, hot sauce, vinegar, oil, and ½ teaspoon each salt and pepper. Measure ½ cup of this mixture and set aside.

In a blender, pulse the remaining veggies with the avocado until the mixture is creamy and smooth. Season to taste with additional salt and pepper. For a more acidic soup, add another dash of vinegar.

Refrigerate for several hours before serving. Top each portion of soup with a spoonful of the reserved chopped veggies and a dollop of Greek yogurt.

Fanfare Tip

Feeling fancy? Sprinkle a pinch of fresh crabmeat over this chilled tomatoey mixture. Feeling spunky? Prepare this as a soup-shooter-style party app and quiz your friends on the secret ingredient (avocado) that smooth-ifies the soup. Winner gets . . . more soup.

Creamy Roasted Asparagus and Mint Soup

Bright, refreshing mint and warm, savory asparagus come together in one pot to create this luxurious yet light soup. The ingredients are pureed until smooth and then whisked with tart lemon juice and half-and-half to create a silky, sweet mouthfeel.

2 pounds asparagus, ends trimmed, halved
3 tablespoons olive oil
Kosher salt and coarse black pepper
1 tablespoon unsalted butter
1 large leek, white and light green parts only, chopped

1 box (32 ounces) lower-sodium vegetable stock
¼ cup chopped fresh mint
¼ cup half-and-half
2 tablespoons fresh lemon juice

Preheat the oven to 400°F.

On a baking sheet, toss the asparagus with 2 tablespoons of the olive oil and season generously with salt and pepper. Roast until lightly browned and very tender, 15 to 18 minutes.

In a large soup pot, heat the remaining 1 tablespoon olive oil and the butter over medium heat. Add the leeks, season with salt and pepper, and cook until translucent, about 3 minutes. Add the roasted asparagus, vegetable stock, and mint. Bring the mixture to a low boil and cook for 1 minute.

Reduce the heat to low. Using an immersion blender (or transferring the soup to a stand blender), pulse until smooth. Let the soup simmer for 15 minutes.

Whisk in the half-and-half and lemon juice. Simmer for an additional 5 minutes and then season to taste with salt and pepper and serve hot.

Fanfare Tip

For a stunning presentation, a contrast of colors is needed. Top this vibrant green broth with a bright dollop of crème fraîche and a handful of golden brown croutons.

Kale and Parmesan Soup

As much as I love a hearty, tummy-warming bowl of broccoli cheddar, all that cream and butter can be a little heavy on the hips. In this light yet comforting soup, tender veggies and wilted kale are immersed in a bath of parmesan-infused broth. How do I squeeze this cheese's noteworthy nuttiness into the pot without adding pounds of parm?

It's all in the rind.

1 tablespoon olive oil
1 tablespoon unsalted butter
1 large leek, white and light green parts only, chopped
1 medium clove garlic, minced
½ cup diced celery
2 teaspoons herbes de Provence or dried thyme
Kosher salt and coarse black pepper

¼ cup dry white wine
6 cups lower-sodium vegetable stock
2 x 2-inch piece of thick parmesan rind
½ teaspoon grated lemon zest
3 large kale leaves (a tender variety like lacinato, a.k.a. Dino), ribs removed and roughly chopped
¼ cup grated parmesan cheese

In a large soup pot, heat the olive oil and butter over medium heat. Add the leek, garlic, celery, herbes de Provence, ½ teaspoon salt, and ¼ teaspoon pepper and cook until the leeks are translucent, 3 to 4 minutes. Increase the heat to high and cook for 1 minute longer. Pour in the white wine and scrape up any browned bits from the bottom. Add the stock and bring to a boil. Once the soup boils, reduce the heat to low, add the parmesan rind, and simmer for 30 minutes.

Increase the heat to medium, stir in the lemon zest, kale, and grated parmesan, and cook until the kale is wilted, 8 to 10 minutes. Season to taste with salt and pepper.

Fanfare Tip

For a sneaky way to slide this healthy soup into a finicky eater's belly, pulse the broth into a puree so that the kale leaves disappear into a stream of green. Sauté some salty bacon for a crunchy topping so the smokiness disguises the "nutritious flavor" of the kale.

Lemony Veggie and Couscous Soup

Soups aren't just a comfort for a bad day or a case of the sniffles. You'll crave a simmering pot of this light, lemony broth—featuring spring veggies, fresh herby dill, and fluffy pasta—healthy, sick, happy, or sad. Serve with a side of gooey grilled cheese and *Law & Order* reruns.

1 tablespoon olive oil
1 tablespoon unsalted butter
1 medium shallot, thinly sliced
1 medium clove garlic, minced
⅓ pound zucchini, sliced into
    ½-inch-thick rounds
⅓ pound yellow squash, sliced into
    ½-inch-thick rounds

Kosher salt and coarse black pepper
2 tablespoons dry white wine
3 cups lower-sodium vegetable stock
⅓ cup couscous
1 teaspoon grated lemon zest
2 tablespoons chopped fresh dill

In a large pot, heat the olive oil and butter over medium heat. Add the shallot, garlic, zucchini, squash, ½ teaspoon each salt and pepper and cook until the shallots are translucent, 2 to 4 minutes. Pour in the wine and scrape up any browned bits from the bottom. Add the vegetable stock and bring to a boil.

Once the soup is boiling, reduce the heat to medium-low and simmer for 15 minutes. Add the couscous and cook, stirring occasionally, for an additional 3 minutes.

Remove the pot from the heat, cover, and let sit for 3 minutes. Stir in the lemon zest and dill. Season to taste with salt and pepper.

Fanfare Tip

Couscous not filling you up? Delve into other distinctive pastas for a more substantial meal. Try out Israeli couscous for the same round shape in a larger form or rice-shaped orzo for a heartier soup. Add an extra cup of stock, as these varieties will soak up a bit more liquid than the couscous.

Spicy Pulled Chicken and Roasted Garlic Soup

SERVES 4

This tomatoey take on chicken tortilla soup is fired up with cayenne and red pepper flakes and cut with the nutty sweetness of roasted garlic. Don't be scared—it'll only tingle your taste buds with heat, as the spice hits the back of your mouth and leaves your tongue free to enjoy the rich, savory flavors.

6 cloves Roasted Garlic (page 225)
2 tablespoons olive oil
1 small sweet onion, thinly sliced
 (about 1 cup)
½ cup chopped celery
2 small jalapeños, ★ seeded and diced
1 teaspoon paprika
½ teaspoon cayenne pepper
½ teaspoon red pepper flakes
1 tablespoon tomato paste
3 cups lower-sodium chicken stock
1 can (14 ounces) diced fire-roasted
 tomatoes

1 can (15 ounces) cannellini beans, drained
 and rinsed
Kosher salt and coarse black pepper
3 cups shredded chicken (white and
 dark meat)
2 tablespoons chopped fresh oregano

GARNISH

1 cup grated parmesan cheese
2 avocados, diced
Lime wedges

★ At Boondini's (our hometown sub hub), my dad made their rich, tomato-based chicken soup with a trace of Mexican spice a staple of our weekend takeout order. He would pop the plastic lid off the crimson-splashed Styrofoam cup and dot the mellow soup with fiery hot sauce. The sudden sting of peppers mingling with shredded chicken and garlic would tickle the air, and I couldn't help but grab a second spoon. In my present-day salute to this soup, I maintain the main players—chicken, tomatoes, and veggies—but triple the heat at the base with diced jalapeños, cayenne, and a pungent punch from red pepper flakes.

Using the flat side of your knife, mash the roasted garlic until it becomes a paste.

In a large soup pot, heat the olive oil over medium heat. Add the onion, celery, jalapeños, paprika, cayenne, and pepper flakes and cook until the onion is translucent, 4 to 5 minutes. Add the tomato paste and roasted garlic, whisk to combine, and cook for 1 minute. Add the chicken stock, canned tomatoes, beans, 1 teaspoon salt, and ½ teaspoon pepper.

Using an immersion blender, pulse several times so that some of the soup is pureed (or puree about one-third of the soup in a stand blender and return it to the pot). This will thicken the whole soup overall.

Bring the soup to a boil and then reduce the heat to medium-low. Cover the soup and simmer, stirring occasionally, for 20 minutes to marry the flavors.

Add the chicken and oregano and stir well to combine. Cook the soup for 5 more minutes to heat the chicken through. Season to taste with salt and pepper and then divide among bowls. Garnish each bowl with parmesan, diced avocado, and lime wedges.

Fanfare Tip

To ease the spice, instead of finishing with parmesan, swirl in a spoonful of creamy Greek yogurt or tangy sour cream.

Wild Mushroom and Eggplant Soup with Coconut and Lemongrass

SERVES 2 TO 4

Hello, my name is Fanny, and I love lemongrass. A bold statement, I know, but it had to be said. The fragrant citrusy flavor runs throughout this velvety soup made up of earthy mushrooms, aromatic roasted eggplant, sweet onions, and creamy coconut milk.

2 cups lower-sodium vegetable stock

1 ounce dried wild mushrooms (such as porcini or oyster)

1 large eggplant (about 1½ pounds), peeled and cut into ½-inch cubes

1 small sweet onion, roughly chopped

3 tablespoons olive oil

Kosher salt and coarse black pepper

1 teaspoon minced fresh ginger

1 medium clove garlic, minced

2 teaspoons grated or minced fresh lemongrass

½ cup canned coconut milk

GARNISH

½ cup sour cream or plain Greek yogurt

¼ cup roughly chopped fresh cilantro

In a saucepan, heat the vegetable stock over high heat.

Place the dried mushrooms in a large, deep heatproof bowl. Once the stock boils, pour it over the dried mushrooms, cover the bowl with a kitchen towel, and let the mushrooms steep for 25 to 30 minutes. Remove the rehydrated mushrooms with a slotted spoon,

Fanfare Tips

- For an artsy presentation, place the sour cream in a plastic bag and cut a very small snip off the bottom corner. Swirl or dot the sour cream on top of the soup to create an elegant pattern. To kick the presentational pizzazz up one more notch, sauté some fresh shiitake mushrooms in butter and scatter them over the top of your creamy design.
- Birds of a feather flock together, and lemongrass goes best with more lemongrass (or something like that). For an exotic lunch combo, pair this earthy, citrusy soup with Ginger and Lemongrass Shrimp Summer Rolls (page 98).

roughly chop, and set aside. Strain the mushroom stock through a fine sieve to get rid of any dirt and then return it to the bowl.

Preheat the oven to 400°F.

On a large baking sheet, toss the eggplant and onion with 2 tablespoons of the olive oil and season with ½ teaspoon salt and ¼ teaspoon pepper. Roast until the veggies are tender and lightly golden, 18 to 20 minutes.

Add the roasted eggplant and onions to the bowl with the stock. Using an immersion blender (or transferring to a blender or food processor), pulse the veggies with the stock until smooth.

In a large soup pot, heat the remaining 1 tablespoon olive oil over medium heat. Add the ginger, garlic, lemongrass, and rehydrated mushrooms and season with salt and pepper. Cook until very fragrant, about 1 minute. Pour the stock mixture into the pot and reduce the heat to medium-low. Simmer the soup, stirring occasionally, for 20 minutes to blend the flavors.

Stir in the coconut milk and simmer for 5 minutes longer. Season the soup to taste with salt and pepper and then divide among bowls. Garnish each bowl with sour cream and cilantro.

Chapter 3

The App Store

Peace out, store-bought cubed cheese platter. Prepare yourself for a voyage into a land where homemade appetizers nearly steal the show. A world where fried shallots and crisp radishes mingle, and traditional salads transform into elegant quesadillas. These starters are more than snacks—they're an epic preview of what's to come.

Baked Veggie Falafel with Gorgonzola Tzatziki

I have a falafel addiction. A falafeldiction, if you will. I can't get enough of these crunchy, herby patties. This recipe takes the falafel out of the fryer and into the oven. Humming with bright parsley and smoky scallions, it's the aromatic veggies and grassy herbs that give them their light, savory flavor. A tangy tzatziki infused with Gorgonzola makes them unlike any falafel you'll ever find.

Perfect for falafeldicts everywhere (just don't call them that to their face).

1 bunch scallions, white and light green parts only, roughly chopped
1 small sweet onion, roughly chopped
1 small shallot, roughly chopped
6 tablespoons olive oil
Kosher salt and coarse black pepper
2 cans (15 ounces each) chickpeas (garbanzo beans), drained and rinsed
Grated zest and juice of 1 lemon

¼ cup chopped cilantro
¼ cup chopped fresh parsley
2 small cloves garlic
1½ teaspoons ground cumin
½ teaspoon ground coriander
½ teaspoon cayenne pepper
1 teaspoon paprika
½ cup Gorgonzola Tzatziki (page 224)

Preheat the oven to 425°F.

In a large bowl, toss the scallions, onion, and shallot with 2 tablespoons of the olive oil and season them generously with salt and pepper. Spread the veggies onto a baking sheet and roast until they are lightly golden and beginning to caramelize, 15 to 20 minutes. Cool to room temperature.

Flippidy-Doo

These falafel make fantastic appetizers, but I'm a fan of bringing them to the dinner table. Transform them into a wholesome vegetarian meal by using an enormous Greek salad of chunky tomatoes, feta, olives, and cucumbers as the base. Slice some creamy avocado into the mix for a dose of healthy fats and drizzle on the Olive Vinaigrette (page 166) from my Rustic Panzanella.

Leave the oven on but reduce the temperature to 400°F.

In a food processor, combine the roasted veggies, chickpeas, lemon zest, lemon juice, cilantro, parsley, garlic, cumin, coriander, cayenne, and paprika. Pulse the mixture a few times until it is smooth but still has some texture. Season to taste with salt and pepper.

To form the falafel, use a ¼-cup scoop and form the mixture into patties. Arrange them on a nonstick baking sheet. Evenly drizzle the falafel with 2 tablespoons of the olive oil.

Bake for 15 minutes. Carefully (they may still be somewhat wet) flip over each patty. Drizzle them with the remaining 2 tablespoons olive oil and bake until they are golden brown, about 15 minutes. Let the falafel cool for 5 minutes before serving, as they will continue to set and harden up out of the oven.

Top each falafel with a spoonful of Gorgonzola Tzatziki.

My Big Fat Hummus Addiction

One evening a week, like clockwork, my mom would bring home a container of the world's smoothest, most inexplicably velvety hummus from Neomonde, a small café in my Carolina hometown that serves Lebanese-inspired fare. Before dinner, we would congregate around it in the kitchen, admiring its glistening olive oil crest and dunking all kinds of crackers within its lemony pool of love.

Dad sharing secrets with
a flight of falafel.

While my sister and I no longer live at home to participate in the habitual hummus hoopla, my family has reinvented the ritual all the way across the Pacific Ocean. Once a year the four of us rendezvous on Oahu, my sister's current home, and during our two-week stay we make multiple visits to The Fat Greek (a homey BYOB café serving Mediterranean fare). We feast on exotic kebabs, tart tzatziki, buttery pita, fluffy falafel, and a chickpea dip so good it could make a Samoan cry. Each lemon-dressed, whipped bite whirls me back to childhood, where one extraordinary night a week—hummus was home.

★ **Baked Veggie Falafel with Gorgonzola Tzatziki** (page 74): Floral parsley and vibrant lemon zest add lightness to these tangy tzatziki-topped, veggie-filled patties.

★ **Chickpea, Fennel, and Mint Salad** (page 162): As an ode to hummus, I like to rewind the chickpea to its original form and enjoy it as the star of this anise-scented, herbaceous salad featuring bright mint and sharp, briny feta.

Strawberry and Goat Cheese Crostini with Vanilla-Balsamic Reduction

Strawberries deserve to be in the spotlight more often. In this extraordinary crostini creation, I promote this fruit from a cameo to the main attraction. Topped with a syrupy balsamic reduction with a subtle hint of vanilla, torn fresh basil, and robust cracked pepper, the crostini are a colorful portrayal of berries at their best.

1 baguette (18 inches long), cut crosswise into 24 equal slices
2 tablespoons unsalted butter, melted
Kosher salt and cracked black pepper
1½ cups chopped strawberries

½ cup plus 2 tablespoons balsamic vinegar
1 teaspoon pure vanilla extract
⅓ cup chopped pistachios
12 ounces goat cheese
½ cup packed fresh basil leaves

Preheat the oven to 400°F.

Spread out the baguette slices on a baking sheet, drizzle them with the melted butter, and season with salt and pepper. Bake until lightly golden brown, 6 to 8 minutes.

In a large bowl, toss the strawberries with 2 tablespoons of the balsamic vinegar. Let them marinate at room temperature while you prepare the rest of the ingredients.

In a small saucepan, combine the remaining ½ cup balsamic vinegar and the vanilla. Bring to a simmer over medium heat and cook, stirring occasionally to keep from burning, until the liquid has reduced by about half and it becomes thick and syrupy, 8 to 10 minutes. Immediately remove the pan from the heat.

In a dry small skillet, toast the pistachios over medium-low heat, tossing frequently, until lightly golden and very fragrant, about 5 minutes. Immediately remove the nuts from the pan and transfer to a bowl to stop the cooking process.

To assemble the crostini, spread each baguette toast with goat cheese and arrange them on a platter. Evenly sprinkle the strawberries and the pistachios over the crostini and gently tear the basil leaves over top. Drizzle the entire platter with the vanilla-balsamic reduction and garnish with cracked black pepper.

Fanfare Tip

For another sweet twist on dessert crostini, spread your buttery baguette slices with a smooth, tangy cheese like Taleggio and top with blueberries and bright, fragrant thyme.

Roasted Veggie Crostini with Sunflower Seed–Cream Cheese Pesto

MAKES 24 CROSTINI

Adding a dollop of cream cheese to your pesto is the perfect way to stretch its substance. It also produces a wonderfully creamy spread. Savory roasted chopped veggies sit atop this smooth pesto crostini, and bold, syrupy reduced balsamic rounds out the flavors and makes for an elegant presentation.

½ **pound zucchini, cut into ¼-inch dice**
½ **pound yellow squash, cut into ¼-inch dice**
1 **small red onion, slivered**
¼ **cup olive oil**
2 **teaspoons dried oregano**
Kosher salt and coarse black pepper

1 **baguette (18 inches long), cut crosswise into 24 equal slices**
½ **cup balsamic vinegar**
Sunflower Seed–Cream Cheese Pesto (page 216)
½ **cup crumbled feta cheese**

Preheat the oven to 400°F.

On a baking sheet, toss the zucchini, squash, and red onion with 2 tablespoons of the oil, the oregano, and ½ teaspoon each salt and pepper. Roast, tossing once halfway through, until tender, 13 to 15 minutes.

Spread the baguette slices on a separate baking sheet, drizzle them with the remaining 2 tablespoons oil, and season with salt and pepper. Bake until lightly golden and crunchy, 6 to 8 minutes.

In a small saucepan, heat the balsamic vinegar over medium-high heat. Once it boils, reduce the heat to medium low and cook, stirring occasionally to keep from burning, until the liquid has become thick and syrupy, 8 to 10 minutes. Immediately remove the pan from the heat.

To assemble the crostini, spread each toasted baguette slice with the pesto and arrange them on a platter. Evenly sprinkle the roasted vegetables over the crostini and then top with the crumbled feta. Drizzle the entire platter with the balsamic reduction.

Flippidy-Doo

For an epic pizza night without the delivery fee, swap in buttery naan bread or pita for the crostini. Paint the flatbread with olive oil and hit it with your best shot of Italian herbs. Throw it on the grill or griddle until lightly charred and crisp and proceed with your pesto, veggies, and feta. Cut into wedges and finish with the balsamic drizzle and a round of craft beers.

BLT Crostini with Whiskey Bacon Jam

MAKES 24 CROSTINI

This nibbly bit of an appetizer turns the old-school BLT into a new-school sensation. Bright, juicy balsamic-scented heirloom tomatoes cut through fatty spiked bacon jam for a brilliantly balanced bite. Also, did I mention bacon jam?

Bacon jam.

1 cup Whiskey Bacon Jam (page 221)
1 pound multicolored heirloom tomatoes (baby or regular size), diced (about 1½ cups)
3 tablespoons olive oil
1 tablespoon balsamic vinegar

1 teaspoon dried oregano
Kosher salt and cracked black pepper
1 baguette (18 inches long), cut crosswise into 24 equal slices
1 cup packed fresh basil leaves

Prepare the Whiskey Bacon Jam and set aside to cool to room temperature.

In a large bowl, toss the tomatoes with 1 tablespoon of the olive oil, the balsamic vinegar, oregano, and a generous pinch each of salt and pepper. Allow the tomatoes to marinate for at least 30 minutes in the fridge.

Preheat the oven to 400°F.

Spread the baguette slices on a baking sheet, drizzle with the remaining 2 tablespoons olive oil, and season with salt and pepper. Bake until lightly golden brown, 6 to 8 minutes.

To assemble the crostini, spread each toasted baguette slice with bacon jam and arrange on a platter. Carefully spoon the marinated tomatoes over the crostini. Tear the basil leaves over top and garnish with additional cracked black pepper.

Fanfare Tip

For a thriftier version of this dish, swap out the baby heirlooms for a juicy, yet less expensive, small tomato variety like cherry or grape.

Beet Salad Stacks with Crispy Shallots

This eccentric hors d'oeuvre unravels a traditional beet salad and pieces it back together in a striking one-bite appetizer with crispy radishes, honeyed goat cheese, and quick-fried shallots. A light orange vinaigrette gives these ruby-colored towers a bright finish.

½ pound small, even-size red beets, peeled and cut into ¼-inch-thick rounds
2 tablespoons olive oil
1 teaspoon chopped fresh rosemary
Kosher salt and cracked black pepper
3 ounces goat cheese, at room temperature
3 teaspoons honey
1 tablespoon fresh orange juice

½ tablespoon white balsamic vinegar
¼ cup flour
1 teaspoon paprika
⅓ cup neutral oil (such as vegetable, grapeseed, or sunflower)
1 medium shallot, thinly sliced into rings
3 small radishes, sliced into very thin rounds
¼ cup packed fresh basil leaves

Preheat the oven to 400°F.

In a large bowl, toss the beet rounds with 1 tablespoon of the olive oil, the rosemary, and ¼ teaspoon each salt and pepper and spread them onto a baking sheet. Roast the beets until knife-tender, 20 to 25 minutes.

Meanwhile, in a small bowl, combine the goat cheese with 2 teaspoons of the honey and a pinch of black pepper.

In a separate small bowl, whisk together the orange juice, white balsamic, and remaining 1 teaspoon honey. While whisking vigorously, stream in the remaining 1 tablespoon olive oil. Season to taste with salt and pepper. Set the orange vinaigrette aside.

Fanfare Tip

Pair this elegant appetizer with a sparkling rosé Champagne. The fresh, fruity aroma and rich mouthfeel stand up beautifully to the crispy shallots.

In a bowl, toss the flour with the paprika and a pinch each of salt and pepper. Line a plate with paper towels and set next to the stove.

In an 8-inch skillet, heat the neutral oil over medium-high heat. The oil is ready when a small pinch of flour spits and sizzles. Dredge the shallot rings in the flour mixture, shake off the excess, and carefully drop them into the pan. Gently tossing them with a slotted spoon, fry the shallots until they are lightly golden, 30 to 40 seconds. Place them on the paper towels to drain and immediately sprinkle with salt.

To assemble the stacks, spread a small amount of the honeyed goat cheese onto a beet round. Top with a radish slice, a basil leaf, and another beet round. Repeat this layering one more time to complete the stack. Make all the stacks and then arrange them on a platter.

Drizzle the beet stacks with several spoonfuls of the orange vinaigrette and then top each one with a small pinch of crispy shallots. Pierce each one with a thick toothpick and serve immediately.

Flippidy-Doo

Transform this bite back into its original form by skipping the stacking. Fill your favorite salad bowl with peppery arugula and scatter the beet rounds, radishes, basil, and goat cheese on top. Gently toss the greens with the orange vinaigrette, divide onto plates, and garnish each salad with a pinch of fried shallots.

The Wizard of Crab Cakes

The fifth member of my family is a crab cake.

This savory, dill-infused comfort food has always been part of our lives. If we were stranded on a desert island and stumbled upon a crab cake, I genuinely believe that my sister would eat me first to ensure that she could consume the whole thing herself. My dad has perfected the art of crab cakes, and they represent the blissful celebration of the four of us together. This dish holds such colossal significance for our family that the first time I prepared it solo, it was just as momentous as the day I graduated from Hebrew School.

Dear Rabbi Lucy Dinner of Temple Beth Or in Raleigh,

Just kidding. Please don't revoke my latkes.

I remember the evening my parents were caught in traffic, and I was tasked with unaccompanied crab cake duty. "With no help?" I said. "No one around to see if I drink too much wine or dice too much celery or spill Old Bay on the counter?" I thought back to my childhood and pondered the many times I had played seafood sous chef and was put in charge of greens. I remembered standing

Crab cake slider prep for Dad's sixtieth birthday. I'd like to take this opportunity to note that I have the handwriting of a serial killer.

in the kitchen, not much higher than the countertop, gently yanking green strands of dill from their stem and handing them to my dad. Years later as a teenager, sharpened blade in hand, I would trim the grassy herb from its stalk and swiftly run my knife through its frilly leaves.

Back in the present moment, I realized this was not my first rodeo and the chief crab cake officer in me instantly kicked in. It was as if I were a musician suddenly recalling each note of a faded tune. I was dicing leeks and zesting lemons without a care in the world. That night my mom had thirds and used the word "creamy" eight times. I had done well. Fast-forward several months to my dad's sixtieth birthday party in New Jersey. I was asked to cater the twenty-two-person event. The highlight of the menu: a slider-style version of my dad's original recipe. One more jump forward in time, and I'm on national television being asked by Rachael Ray to demonstrate a dish with a story.

In that moment, it occurred to me that it was as if my dad had been teaching me the lessons of life through crab cakes all along. Don't touch anything sharp; a little more credibility here; a little more reliability there. One day you're three feet tall plucking herbs and the next you're on *The Rachael Ray Show*. As does anything in life, it takes time to gain responsibility—and when it comes, it's up to you to decide what to do with it.

I'd like to believe that it brought me here, to this very page.

The following recipe is my homage to our family's comfort food, traditionally served with cocktail sauce.

★ **Dilled Meyer Lemon Crab Cake Sliders** (page 84): These handheld odes to the original are dolloped with roasted tomato aioli—a creamy fusion of acidic tomatoes and sweet, mellow aromatics.

Dilled Meyer Lemon Crab Cake Sliders

Everyone's heart pitter-patters a little when they hear the words "crab cake." There's something comforting about the fusion of savory spices and sweet, tender crab sizzled until crisp. This recipe transforms the traditional entrée into a casual, no-forks-required appetizer. These juicy handheld sliders are packed with fresh dill and tart Meyer lemon and slathered with a rich tomato aioli.

CRAB CAKES

2 tablespoons olive oil

2 leeks, white and light green parts only, diced

2 stalks celery with leafy tops, diced

Kosher salt and coarse black pepper

½ pound jumbo lump crabmeat (see Fanfare Tip), picked over for shells

½ pound lump crabmeat, picked over for shells

3 tablespoons chopped fresh dill

½ tablespoon Old Bay seasoning

Grated zest and juice of 1 Meyer lemon

¼ cup mayonnaise

1¼ cups panko breadcrumbs

About 1 cup neutral oil (such as vegetable, grapeseed, or sunflower), for sautéing

SLIDERS

2 cups baby arugula

1 tablespoon fresh lemon juice

1 tablespoon olive oil

Kosher salt and coarse black pepper

18 slider-size Martin's potato rolls, split open and toasted (or King's Hawaiian Sweet Dinner Rolls)

1 cup Roasted Tomato Aioli (page 223)

Make the crab cakes: In a large skillet, heat the olive oil over medium heat. Add the leeks, celery, and ½ teaspoon each salt and pepper and cook until the veggies become softened, 5 to 7 minutes. Set aside and cool to room temperature.

In a large bowl, gently fold the cooled veggies with the crabmeat, dill, Old Bay, lemon zest, lemon juice, mayonnaise, and ¼ cup of the panko. Season to taste with salt and pepper.

Fanfare Tip

Jumbo lump crabmeat is a bit more expensive than lump, so this half-and-half combo cuts costs while still giving you a nice ratio of the plump, juicy meat.

Spread the remaining 1 cup panko on a plate.

Preheat the oven to 250°F.

To form the patties, use a ¼-cup scoop and shape the mixture into 16 to 18 equally sized, tightly packed mini crab cakes. Carefully coat the outside of each patty in panko.

In a large skillet, working in batches, heat 2 tablespoons neutral oil over medium heat. Without crowding the pan, add the crab cakes and cook until golden brown, 3 to 5 minutes per side. Add more oil as needed for each batch. Transfer the cooked crab cakes to a baking dish and keep warm in the oven while you cook the remaining batches.

Assemble the sliders: Toss the arugula with the lemon juice, olive oil, and a pinch each of salt and pepper. Top each roll bottom with a crab cake, a generous drizzle of aioli, a pinch of the arugula salad, and the top bun.

Flippidy-Doo

Heat up leftover crab cakes for 20 to 25 minutes in a 300°F oven and assemble them open-faced on toasted English muffins. Top with a poached egg, a pinch of arugula, and a splash of the tomato aioli for a coastal-themed breakfast Benedict.

Pear Quesadilla with Balsamic Onions, Gorgonzola, and Walnuts

SERVES 4

Pears in a quesadilla? I promise I'm not crazy. Okay, I can't promise that, but I can guarantee that you'll flip for this sweet and salty salad-esque starter. Stuffed inside a crisp tortilla, juicy pears and tangy balsamic onions balance the bite from sharp, creamy Gorgonzola. Toasted walnuts and a touch of honey will convince you that you've just had dessert.

1 small red onion, thinly sliced

2 tablespoons balsamic vinegar

Kosher salt and coarse black pepper

¼ cup roughly chopped walnuts

2 burrito-size flour tortillas

2 cups baby spinach

½ cup Gorgonzola cheese, ★ crumbled

1 large pear, peeled and thinly sliced

2 tablespoons neutral oil (such as vegetable, grapeseed, or sunflower)

2 tablespoons honey

Preheat the oven to 375°F.

On a baking sheet, toss the red onion with the vinegar and season with salt and pepper. Roast until the onions are tender and lightly caramelized, about 20 minutes.

Reduce the oven temperature to 250°F.

In a dry small skillet, toast the walnuts over medium-low heat, tossing frequently, until lightly golden and very fragrant, about 5 minutes. Immediately remove the nuts from the pan and transfer to a bowl to stop the cooking process.

On one half of each tortilla, evenly layer the balsamic onions, spinach, Gorgonzola, pears, and walnuts. Fold the tortillas over to make a half-moon quesadilla shape.

★ When she graduated from banana yogurt and ravioli, my sister became a salad savant. I remember sharing bites of her favorite green-centric dish. It was a play on the traditional Waldorf salad, mingling juicy pears with sharp, tangy Gorgonzola, sugary roasted nuts, and creamy balsamic. I have dismantled these flavors and layered them back together inside a flour tortilla for my own handheld spin on this classic.

In a large skillet, heat 1 tablespoon of the neutral oil over medium heat. Cook one quesadilla until golden brown and crispy, 2 to 3 minutes per side, then transfer to a baking sheet to keep warm in the oven. Repeat with the remaining quesadilla, using 1 more tablespoon of the neutral oil.

Slice the quesadillas into wedges and evenly drizzle with the honey.

Fanfare Tip

Match the sweet notes of these crispy bites with an acidic, honeyed Riesling.

Flippidy-Doo

Double up on the balsamic onions and use them as a garnish for Pan-Seared Steak with Sage Butter (page 138).

Black Sesame Chicken Satay Kebabs

Peanut butter and coconut go together like, well, peanut butter and jelly. Spice up ordinary chicken kebabs by bathing them in this sweet, tangy Thai sauce. Pass them around as a party pleaser, or gather six friends for a meal. For color and freshness: Crisp asparagus and scallions get skewered along for the ride. For a touch of crunch: black sesame seeds. Chopped peanuts for the win.

2½ pounds boneless skinless chicken breast, cut into 3-inch-long strips about 1 inch wide
¼ cup plain Greek yogurt
2 tablespoons toasted sesame oil
2 teaspoons grated orange zest
Juice of 1 orange
1 tablespoon lower-sodium soy sauce
1 tablespoon rice vinegar
1 teaspoon paprika
Kosher salt and coarse black pepper

2 pounds thick asparagus, ends trimmed, cut crosswise into thirds
2 bunches scallions, white and light green parts only, halved crosswise
2 tablespoons olive oil
Satay Sauce (recipe follows)

GARNISH
¼ cup chopped roasted salted peanuts
1 tablespoon black sesame seeds

In a large bowl, combine the chicken with the Greek yogurt, sesame oil, orange zest, orange juice, soy sauce, rice vinegar, paprika, ½ teaspoon salt, and ¼ teaspoon pepper. Toss well, cover with plastic wrap, and place in the fridge to marinate for at least 1 hour. Meanwhile, soak 25 (12-inch) wooden skewers in water for about 20 minutes.

Preheat a grill★ or grill pan to medium-high.

Toss the asparagus and scallions with the olive oil and season well with salt and pepper.

Growing up with a built-in stovetop grill meant one thing: Kebabs were a constant. The joy behind this meal was its wonderful lack of complexity—protein, veggies, sauce—and the fun of hovering around a smoky grate with my family, no matter the weather. My current kitchen isn't equipped with that feature, so I substitute a good-quality grill pan to achieve those char marks year-round.

Thread about 3 pieces each of asparagus and scallions crosswise onto the skewers. On separate skewers thread the chicken lengthwise so that it's pierced all the way through and won't slide around while grilling (2 to 3 strips per skewer).

Grill each chicken skewer 3 to 5 minutes per side, rotating as necessary to cook each piece evenly. Grill the vegetable skewers until lightly charred, 2 to 4 minutes per side.

Pour half of the satay sauce across the bottom of a large platter. Top with the chicken and veggie skewers and garnish with the chopped peanuts and black sesame seeds. Serve extra satay sauce on the side for dipping.

Satay Sauce

MAKES ABOUT 2½ CUPS

1 tablespoon neutral oil (such as vegetable, grapeseed, or sunflower)
1 large clove garlic, minced
1 tablespoon grated fresh ginger
1½ cups coconut milk
½ cup creamy peanut butter

1 tablespoon lower-sodium soy sauce
½ teaspoon fish sauce
Juice of 1 orange
1 tablespoon honey
Kosher salt and coarse black pepper

In a small saucepan, heat the oil over medium heat. Add the garlic and ginger and cook until very fragrant, about 3 minutes. Add the coconut milk, peanut butter, soy sauce, fish sauce, orange juice, and honey, whisking well to combine. Season to taste with salt and pepper.

Fanfare Tip

For an interactive hors d'oeuvre experience, try serving up an assortment of toppings for your satay. Instead of using the sesame seeds as a garnish, present them in self-serve ramekins along with chopped peanuts, fresh cilantro sprigs, and sliced chilies.

Prosciutto-Stuffed Zucchini Rollatini with Feta and Brown Butter

You know when people say, "That's the stuff dreams are made of"? They're referring to brown butter. I'm a big believer that apps for entertaining should be wildly impressive on the plate and easy behind the scenes. In this flavorful twist on rollatini, briny feta and salty prosciutto are layered together inside rosemary-scented zucchini slices. Splashed with sweet, nutty brown butter, these fantastic hors d'oeuvres might only make it to the party in your mouth.

4 large zucchini (about 2 pounds)
⅓ cup olive oil
2 teaspoons chopped fresh
    rosemary
Kosher salt and cracked black pepper
4 tablespoons unsalted butter

18 thin slices prosciutto
1 cup crumbled feta cheese

GARNISH

1 tablespoon chopped fresh parsley
½ teaspoon grated lemon zest

Preheat the oven to 375°F.

Trim the ends off the zucchini so that they have a flat, sturdy bottom. Stand them up on your cutting board and using a very sharp knife (or mandoline), cut the zucchini lengthwise into 18 strips ⅛ inch thick.

In a small bowl, whisk together the oil and rosemary. Brush both sides of the zucchini slices with the rosemary oil and season with salt and pepper. Arrange the zucchini slices on a baking sheet and roast, flipping each strip halfway through, until tender, 8 to 10 minutes. Set aside to cool.

Flippidy-Doo

Double the rosemary oil, add 1 large clove minced garlic, 2 tablespoons lemon juice to the extra portion and use it as a marinade for grilled chicken.

In a small skillet, melt the butter over low heat. Once the butter is fully melted, increase the heat to medium. Whisking occasionally, keep an eye on the butter as it begins to foam, and then changes from a pale blonde to a golden shade, about 5 minutes. When the butter's aroma becomes very fragrant and nutty and the color is a deep golden tone, remove the pan from the heat.

Season the butter with a pinch of salt, whisk vigorously, and then strain through a fine-mesh sieve to get rid of any dark brown bits.

Lay the cooled zucchini strips on a flat surface and top each one with a thin slice of pro-sciutto. Place 1 scant tablespoon of feta on the bottom of the strips and roll the zucchini closed.

Arrange the rolls seam-side down on a large platter and drizzle them evenly with the brown butter. Garnish with the chopped parsley and lemon zest.

Grilled Vegetable Roll-a-Teenys

MAKES 12 BITE-SIZE ROLLS

Looking for an innovative way to pack big Italian flavors into one *teeny* bite? These oregano-dusted, stacked, and rolled veggies are dolloped with lemony ricotta and are swimming in a sea of lusciously light marinara. Platter up these elegant bites with a spoon so guests can ladle marinara onto their individual rolls. Toast up some garlic bread to go along with any leftover sauce and you've got two apps in one.

1 cup Basil Marinara (page 227) or use
store-bought marinara
3 medium zucchini
3 medium yellow squash
½ cup olive oil
2 teaspoons dried oregano
12 thick asparagus spears
Kosher salt and coarse black pepper

¼ cup ricotta cheese ★
2 tablespoons grated parmesan cheese
1 teaspoon chopped fresh basil, plus
12 large basil leaves
1 teaspoon chopped fresh oregano
½ teaspoon grated lemon zest
1 teaspoon honey

Make the Basil Marinara and keep it covered on low heat while you prepare the rest of the ingredients.

Trim the ends off the zucchini and squash so that they have a flat, sturdy bottom. Stand them upright on your cutting board and using a very sharp knife (or mandoline), cut them lengthwise into strips ⅛ inch thick.

Preheat a grill or grill pan to medium-high.

Whisk together the oil and oregano and brush it onto the zucchini, squash, and asparagus. Season the veggies with salt and pepper. Grill each zucchini and squash strip until tender and slightly charred, about 1 minute per side. Grill the asparagus 2 to 4 minutes, and then trim each spear so only the top 2 inches remain.

★ At Nina's, my family's favorite local Italian bistro in Raleigh, the eggplant rollatini is the dish that keeps driving us back. Stuffed with whipped, fluffy ricotta and floating in a stream of slightly sweet, light-as-air marinara, each savory bite deserves a drumroll. In my miniature mimic of this remarkable meal, I highlight the creamy ricotta with floral herbs and bright lemon zest.

In a small bowl, mix together the ricotta, parmesan, chopped basil, oregano, lemon zest, honey, and salt and pepper to taste.

To assemble the rolls, stack 1 strip of the zucchini and squash on top of each other. On the bottom of the layered veggies, place 1 basil leaf (crosswise), 1 asparagus spear (crosswise), and a dollop of the herbed ricotta. Roll tightly and stand up so the basil leaf and asparagus head poke out of the top. Use additional ricotta as needed to hold the roll together. Repeat with the remaining ingredients until all the rolls are complete.

Pour the marinara onto a large platter and arrange the rolls on top.

Fanfare Tip

While you're already in the herb aisle, grab a handful of chives. Blanch, dry, and transfer them to a blender with ½ cup extra-virgin olive oil and a big pinch of salt. Let the mixture sit for several hours and then press through a fine-mesh sieve. Dot your homemade herb oil along the rim of your roll-a-teeny platter for a bright green zing.

Vegetarian Lettuce Wraps with Sweet and Sour Tomato Vinaigrette

I don't think we wrap enough things in lettuce. Everyone always wants a light, healthy snack, but lettuce wraps somehow tend to get overlooked. Well, start looking. In this nutritious dish, veggies are simply sautéed with bright, grassy parsley and stuffed into a crisp butter lettuce leaf. For drizzling, dipping, or dunking: a slightly sweet, refreshing tomato vinaigrette that packs a burst of acidity from fresh lemon juice.

2 tablespoons neutral oil (such as vegetable, grapeseed, or sunflower)
1 pound zucchini, cut into ½-inch cubes
1 pound yellow squash, cut into ½-inch cubes
1 pound eggplant, peeled and cut into ½-inch cubes

1 small red onion, roughly chopped
Kosher salt and coarse black pepper
¼ cup chopped fresh parsley
2 heads butter (bibb) lettuce
1 cup crumbled feta cheese
Sweet and Sour Tomato Vinaigrette (recipe follows)

In a large deep skillet, heat the oil over medium-high heat. Add the zucchini, squash, eggplant, red onion, ½ teaspoon salt, and ¼ teaspoon pepper and toss to combine. Cook the veggies, stirring occasionally, until crisp-tender and slightly golden on the outside, 8 to 10 minutes. Remove the pan from the heat, season the veggies to taste with salt and pepper, and toss with the parsley.

Separate the butter lettuce leaves and serve alongside the veggies, crumbled feta, and Sweet and Sour Tomato Vinaigrette.

Fanfare Tip

These sautéed vegetables can be served warm, room temperature, or chilled—so take your leaves on the go for a fantastic picnic snack. Pour the veggies and vinaigrette into takeout containers and wrap the washed butter lettuce leaves in paper towels. No utensils required.

Sweet and Sour Tomato Vinaigrette

MAKES 1 CUP

4 small vine-ripened or Roma (plum)
 tomatoes, roughly chopped
1 tablespoon olive oil
Kosher salt and coarse black pepper
1 tablespoon minced shallot

1 tablespoon fresh lemon juice
1 teaspoon honey
1 teaspoon champagne vinegar
2 tablespoons olive oil

Preheat the oven to 400°F.

On a baking sheet, toss the tomatoes with the 1 tablespoon olive oil and season with salt and pepper. Roast until the tomatoes are wilted and slightly darkened, about 20 to 25 minutes.

In a food processor or blender, pulse the roasted tomatoes and their juices with the shallot, lemon juice, honey, and vinegar until smooth. With the motor running, stream in the olive oil until the vinaigrette is thoroughly emulsified. Season to taste with salt and pepper.

Sisterhood of the Traveling Cabbage

I remember the day my dad told me he could travel through time.

He took my hand and led me into the kitchen toward our refrigerator. I squeezed my eyes shut and braced for a chilly and turbulent exodus into the past. I hoped Julia Child or Michael J. Fox would be there on the other side. I returned to reality to find my dad cradling an oversize head of cabbage and a handful of lemons.

He instructed me to fill the enormous pot on the counter with water and locate the sugar in our predominantly organic pantry. As I sat on the floor sifting through cans of tuna and split pea soup in search of the granulated crystals, we slowly began our journey through time. Our travels began with a woman named Fannie. Not the one who's currently typing this book—this is the tale of my great-grandma Fannie for whom I was named. My dad's maternal grandmother was a slight woman with a whimsical spirit and a kind heart. She used to say things like, "If you ever put anything on backwards, like your pants, don't change or you'll be surprised," and "Always go out the same door you came in." In addition to providing my dad with a divine appreciation for life, once a month each winter, she also filled him with stuffed cabbage. The recipe derived from her sister Sara—my sister's namesake—and her original handwritten instructions rested on the counter before us.

Just as the aromas of roasted garlic and rosemary chicken are forever branded onto my soul, the sweet and sour scent of tomatoes simmering with tart lemon is imprinted onto my dad's. After Grandma Fannie passed on, my dad urged his beloved grandfather to tutor him and my mom on this sacred stuffed sensation. Eighty years old but with the comical quirk of a teenager, Poppa George guided my parents through every leaf. He gingerly peered into the crimson pot of tomatoes, sugar, and lemon, as if exposing photos in the darkroom of his

My great-grandparents, Poppa George and Grandma Fannie, "taking the cake" at a party in 1942 after serving Aunt Sara's famous stuffed cabbage recipe. Sara's handwritten recipe (which still exists) concluded with the instruction to put the dish in the oven "and then trust to God."

photography studio, and advised my dad on the importance of thoroughly blending the sauce. Poppa George was an animated man who often liked to talk with his hands. He gestured a stirring motion with the wooden spoon, and then—not realizing the utensil wasn't attached to his body—boldly tossed up his arms as if to say, "You see!" and sent crushed tomatoes catapulting through the air onto the kitchen ceiling.

My dad's laughter drew me back into the present moment, and I looked down to see my hands neatly rolling orange- and herb-perfumed meat into a veiny sheet of boiled cabbage. It suddenly hit me that through his enchanting tale of the original Fannie and Sara three generations back, the Hungarian dish that warmed his stomach and heart, and the time my mom cleaned tomatoes off the ceiling, he had walked me through the entire recipe.

And in that moment I realized that together, we had just traveled through time. Who needs a DeLorean?

★ **Vegetarian Lettuce Wraps with Sweet and Sour Tomato Vinaigrette** (page 94): I swap out the meat-stuffed cabbage for crunchy butter lettuce leaves filled with tender chopped veggies. To mimic the traditional sweet and sour sauce: a light tomato vinaigrette flowing with tart lemon juice and honey.

Ginger and Lemongrass Shrimp Summer Rolls

In need of a light, refreshing bite for your next pool party? No napkins required for these summer rolls, as we're eliminating the fryer and embracing the fresh. Delicate rice paper wrappers are stuffed with raw crunchy goodies like sweet Thai basil and crisp carrot ribbons. Lemongrass-infused shrimp add a citrusy note, and tangy coconut peanut sauce is served alongside for dunking.

18 medium shrimp, shelled and deveined
1 tablespoon fresh lime juice
1 tablespoon toasted sesame oil
1 teaspoon minced fresh ginger
½ teaspoon minced or grated fresh lemongrass
1 teaspoon lower-sodium soy sauce
Kosher salt and coarse black pepper
16 rice paper wrappers (you'll want extra on hand in case several break)

1½ cups pea shoots or bean sprouts
Leaves from 1 bunch fresh Thai or regular basil
Leaves from 1 bunch fresh mint
1 large seedless cucumber, peeled and cut into matchsticks
2 carrots, peeled into ribbons with a vegetable peeler
Coconut Peanut Dipping Sauce (recipe follows)

Preheat the oven to 400°F.

In a large bowl, toss the shrimp with the lime juice, sesame oil, ginger, lemongrass, and soy sauce. Season with a pinch of salt and pepper. Without crowding, arrange them on a baking sheet and roast until the shrimp are opaque in the center, 7 to 8 minutes. Once they are cool enough to handle, cut them into thirds.

Set out an assembly line of ingredients starting with the rice paper wrappers, a large platter of warm water, and a damp, outspread kitchen towel. Next, set up the shrimp, pea shoots, basil, mint, cucumber, and carrots. Place a serving platter at the end for the finished rolls.

Submerge a rice paper wrapper into the warm water until it's pliable, 5 to 10 seconds. Carefully transfer the outspread wrapper to the damp towel. Dividing equally (to ensure you have enough for the total number of rolls), layer the fillings across the lower third of the wrapper. Fold in the sides (like a burrito) and then roll away from you until the edges are sealed. Transfer the wrapped summer roll to the serving platter and repeat until all the rolls are complete.

Serve immediately or prepare up to 1 hour ahead and store in the fridge until serving. If making the rolls ahead of time, layer each level with a damp paper towel so they don't stick together. Remove the paper towels before serving. Serve with the dipping sauce.

Coconut Peanut Dipping Sauce

MAKES ¾ CUP

1 small clove garlic, minced
1 teaspoon minced fresh ginger
¼ cup creamy peanut butter
¼ cup canned unsweetened coconut milk

2 tablespoons fresh orange juice
1 tablespoon soy sauce
1 teaspoon honey
Kosher salt

In a blender or food processor, pulse the garlic, ginger, peanut butter, coconut milk, orange juice, soy sauce, and honey until very smooth. Season to taste with salt.

Fanfare Tips

- Trade the shrimp for silky avocado slices to create a vegetarian version of this appetizer that's packed with nutritious ingredients.
- For a fall twist on these fresh rolls, exchange the shrimp and cucumber for seasonal ingredients like roasted pumpkin cubes and pomegranate seeds.

Coconut-Kissed Calamari with Lime-Agave Dip

Homemade calamari is only intimidating if you let it be—or if you're afraid of squid. In which case, flip the page. For those of you who stuck around, shake the nearest palm tree because we're giving this seafood appetizer an island-style twist. Juicy calamari are soaked in buttermilk, quick-fried to perfection, and sprinkled with a nutty toasted coconut "dust." Instead of traditional marinara, drag these crunchy rings through a refreshing citrus and agave dip.

¾ cup unsweetened coconut flakes
1 pound cleaned squid, tubes and
   tentacles cut into ⅓-inch-thick rings
1 cup buttermilk
Canola oil, for deep-frying (enough to be
   3 to 4 inches deep in your pot)

1 cup all-purpose flour
Kosher salt
½ teaspoon cracked black pepper
Lime wedges, for serving
Lime-Agave Dip (recipe follows)

Preheat the oven to 350°F.

Spread the coconut flakes on a small baking sheet and bake, keeping a very close eye as it burns easily, until lightly golden, 3 to 5 minutes. Allow the toasted coconut flakes to cool to room temperature, then transfer them to a food processor and pulse until they become a very fine dust.

Soak the squid in the buttermilk for 20 minutes.

Pour enough canola oil into a Dutch oven or large deep pot to come up 3 to 4 inches. Heat the oil to 360°F.

In a large bowl, combine the flour, ½ teaspoon salt, and the pepper. Working in about 3 batches so you don't crowd the oil, remove the squid from the buttermilk, shake off the excess, dredge them in the flour, and carefully add them to the oil. Fry the squid until lightly golden yellow and crisp, about 1 minute. With a spider or slotted spoon, transfer the fried calamari to paper towels to drain. Sprinkle them immediately with the toasted coconut dust and salt.

Serve with lime wedges and Lime-Agave Dip.

Lime-Agave Dip

MAKES ¾ CUP

½ cup plain Greek yogurt
¼ teaspoon grated lime zest
1 tablespoon fresh lime juice

2 teaspoons agave
Kosher salt

In a small bowl, whisk together the yogurt, lime zest, lime juice, and agave. Season to taste with salt.

Flippidy-Doo

Fry up some tail-on shrimp and shower them in coconut dust for another simple seafood starter. Serve the shrimp with a mixture of ½ cup orange marmalade, ¼ cup Dijon mustard, and the juice of 1 lime for a quick zesty sauce.

The Dinner Question

Dinnertime conversation at our house began with the usual banter. How was your day? What did you eat for lunch? How did you convince your math teacher to raise your grade to a D?

Without fail, the chatter always circled around to the trusty Dinner Question. Each night—somewhere between dabbing the gravy off his shirt and hand-feeding swordfish to the cats—my dad would say, "Okay, so for tonight's dinner question . . ." He would trail off into a thoughtful meditation, and my mom and sister and I would exchange excited glances. I would immediately organize my thoughts and ponder intricate queries such as: "If you had a tail, which type of tail would you choose and why?"*

Other than eating, this was our most treasured around-the-table pastime. None of us was interested in sports, so this game was our principal form of mealtime entertainment. It also served as the quickest way to retrieve personal information from the most current boyfriend who thought he was just coming by for crab cakes. This really helped narrow down my prom dates.

Of all the questions asked and of all the responses returned, one particular evening's dialogue stuck with me. "You can bring three things, and only three things, to an island," my dad said. "Any three things you like. What are they?" Without hesitation and nearly taking flight toward the ceiling, my mom leapt from her seat and shouted one word at the top of her lungs.

"Avocados!"

Yes, all three of her survival elements were avocados. I was well aware of my mom's passion for this mysterious fruit—hence the twelve avocados currently ripen-

---

*And in case you were wondering: I would choose a capuchin monkey's tail because it serves as an extra limb and would have come in handy while typing this book.

ing in a nearby bowl—but it was in this moment I began to pay attention. As she sang the praises of their limitless health benefits, their luxuriously creamy flavor and endless versatility, I looked down at the luminous green chunks scattered throughout the salad she had made. I wouldn't necessarily swap an avocado for the six-pack of beer I was bringing to my imaginary island retreat . . . but I certainly saw it in a new light.

It was this very day on earth that I was certain my mom would climb into her spaceship and head back to where she came from.

This story epitomizes my mom's remarkable influence on my current kitchen. Without her mapping out the edible world of natural, organic foods for me, I might have spent my entire childhood glued to Cool Ranch Doritos and sheltered from wholesome ingredients. By sheltered I mean: under the kitchen table feeding the frisée on my plate to our cats. She was the visionary in our family who patiently steered us toward the healing power of green cuisine, raw foods, and eating wisely to nourish and balance the body inside and out.

Inspired by her love affair with avocados, I began to wedge them into sandwiches and blend them into smoothies. One day, I even decided to make my very first guacamole. The rest is history.

★ **Soon-to-Be-Famous Already Famous Guacamole** (page 104): I squeeze in a healthy dose of lime juice and add finely chopped sharp onion and jalapeño to give the silky avocados a zestful zip.

Soon-to-Be-Famous Already Famous Guacamole

This appetizer was once requested four times in one month—and not for my catering business. It was summertime and cookout-style gatherings in the neighborhood courtyard became a weekend tradition. If there had been a bouncer on the lawn each Saturday, this guacamole would have repeatedly trumped Paris Hilton at the velvet ropes. My rustic recipe has the perfect balance of lime, salt, and crunch. Crisp onions, jalapeños, and a hint of garlic are what give this dip its depth, and a splash of olive oil makes it glisten.

2 avocados
Juice of 1 lime
½ cup chopped Roma (plum) tomatoes (2 small)
1 tablespoon finely diced red onion
1 small jalapeño, seeded and finely diced

1 small clove garlic, minced
2 tablespoons chopped fresh cilantro
1 tablespoon olive oil
Kosher salt
¼ teaspoon coarse black pepper

Halve the avocados lengthwise and remove the pit by carefully rapping it with a knife (so the blade wedges into it) and twisting to remove. Discard the pit. Use a spoon to remove the avocado's flesh and place it into a large bowl. Use a fork to gently break up the avocado, leaving it in mostly chunky pieces.

Add the lime juice, tomatoes, red onion, jalapeño, garlic, cilantro, oil, ¼ teaspoon salt, and the black pepper. Fold the ingredients together with the fork, making sure not to overmash the avocado. Season to taste with more salt and serve immediately.

Flippidy-Doo

Use this creamy guac for dolloping instead of dipping. Give it a whirl on Pulled Buffalo Chicken Tacos with Red Onions and Poblanos (page 122) to smooth out the spicy notes of the hot sauce.

Fanfare Tip

If you can't easily make a dent in the avocado's dark skin with your finger, it's not ready for its guacamole close-up. The texture of an unripe avocado will be tough and the flavor unpleasant. Let the firm ones ripen on your counter for a few days, or if you're on the verge of a guacemergency, put them in a closed paper bag to speed up the process.

Garlic and Herb-Infused Dipping Oil

No reservations required for this restaurant-style before-dinner dip. All you need are a few handfuls of herbs, a couple garlic cloves, and a good-quality oil to craft this landing pad for warm, crusty bread. For a real kick, double the red pepper flakes.

1 cup extra-virgin olive oil
6 medium cloves garlic, gently smashed but still intact
6 sprigs fresh thyme

4 sprigs fresh rosemary
½ teaspoon red pepper flakes
½ teaspoon dried oregano
½ teaspoon kosher salt

In a small saucepan, stir together the oil, garlic, thyme, rosemary, pepper flakes, oregano, and salt. Set the pan over medium heat, and when the garlic cloves begin to sizzle, turn the heat down to medium-low and simmer for 20 minutes, removing the garlic cloves when they turn golden brown, about 15 minutes. (The cloves may stay in for the full 20 minutes as long as they don't get any darker than golden brown.)

Cool to room temperature before serving and leave herbs and garlic in for presentation.

Flippidy-Doo's

- Use leftover garlic oil to sauté some shrimp, drizzle over crispy roasted potatoes, or whisk with lemon as a tangy marinade for lamb chops.
- Smear the flavored oil onto crusty ciabatta and melt on some parmesan for a garlic-bread-like accompaniment to Crispy Baked Chicken Parmesan with Fresh Mozzarella (page 118).

The Unhappy Camper

The expression "happy camper" was extinguished when I attended my first sleep-away adventure at age nine.

I was homesick and sarcastic and had no interest in constructing a feather headband. Unfortunately I had begged my parents to let me join this monthlong sailboating, s'mores-making escapade, so my letters home disclosing how the counselors were trying to brainwash me were rather ineffective.

As the days dragged on and my morale continued to decline—*What nine-year-old from the suburbs of Raleigh needs an archery certification?!*—I began to ponder what had brought me there in the first place. It certainly wasn't the equestrian program or the canoeing or the wheel-thrown pottery. It was the years of encouraging stories from my immediate family about their positive experiences at summer camp. For my mom: It was the buttery deep-fried French toast—so life-altering that to this day it is still tucked away in a scrapbook (see "The Museum of Breakfast," page 40). For my dad: the unforgettable friendship with Jamie Farber, with whom he once cooked salami in a dustpan over the flames of a trashcan in their bunk. For my sister: the endless supply of gooey toasted grilled cheese and silky tomato soup for dipping.

That was it. Everyone's memories revolved around food, while I was busy gluing glitter onto a stick. Fortunately, one day a care package arrived in the mail from back home. I assumed it was a clipping of our Persian cat's fur or some sort of machine that would teleport me home. Instead, what I found inside was a blue and yellow tin of sugary honey-roasted nuts. Just at that moment, the counselors' peppy, rhythmic voices echoed over the intercom. It was time for teamwork building. I sank into my mattress and pretended to be invisible. *I succeeded.* Finally alone, I popped the lid off the canister and smelled the buttery aroma of

A photo my sister and I sent our parents from camp. I attached a note that began, "Dear Mom and Dad, send help. You have until Sunday, and then I walk the three hours home in the moccasins I made here during arts and crafts."

peanuts—roasted, salty, and caramelized to perfection. In that moment I knew that this snack had forever stolen my summer, and my heart.

In my kitchen today, I fiddle with a sprinkle of cayenne or a splash of maple. But one bite of these classic, familiar honey-roasted peanuts and the possibilities are endless. No one can tell me what to do or which certification is missing from my Land and Sea Manual. Hand over the whistle—Fanny's in charge now.

You're dismissed.

★ **Honey-Roasted Rosemary and Black Pepper Peanuts** (page 108): Dusted with piney rosemary and sharp kicks of pepper, these are a grown-up spin on the classic original.

Honey-Roasted Rosemary and Black Pepper Peanuts

Roasting your own nuts seems intimidating, but it's easier than you think. Sure, you can go store-bought, but where's the fun in that? This recipe hauls Mr. Peanut out of the tin can and into your oven. That sounded slightly more homicidal than I meant it.

Still not convinced? Crafting your snacks from scratch gives you the upper hand to season as you wish. I like mine with woody rosemary and spicy bursts of coarse black pepper.

1 tablespoon unsalted butter, melted

1 tablespoon honey

2 teaspoons finely chopped fresh rosemary

1 cup salted roasted peanuts

1½ tablespoons light brown sugar

¼ teaspoon coarse black pepper

Kosher salt

Preheat the oven to 350°F.

In a small bowl, whisk together the melted butter, honey, and rosemary. Add the peanuts and toss to coat. Spread the peanuts in an even layer on a nonstick baking sheet and roast, tossing every 5 minutes, until golden brown, 15 to 18 minutes.

Immediately toss the nuts with the brown sugar, pepper, and a pinch of salt. Once they have cooled, season to taste with additional salt and pepper if necessary.

Fanfare Tip

Go nuts with your nuts. Start with the simple base of peanuts and melted butter and add your favorite seasonings from there. For a smoky bar snack, try a dash of Worcestershire and a shake of smoked sea salt. For a sweet treat perfect for family movie night, cinnamon sugar does the trick.

Chapter 4

EntréePreneur

It's time for the main attraction, and the substantial superstars in this section are served home-style with a sophisticated spin and a sprinkle of comfort.

Meatless Monday Angel Hair with Burst Tomatoes and Goat Cheese

SERVES 4

As much as I love spending hours preparing an impressive meal, sometimes I just want a quick dinner that's ready in time to sit down and watch *Jeopardy!* In this unfussy vegetarian entrée, juicy tomatoes are roasted until they pop and then tossed with a splash of white wine and tangy goat cheese to create a light sauce that bonds to thin strands of angel hair. So tasty and sophisticated you'll be shocked at how quickly it hits the plate.

3 cups whole small tomatoes (such as cherry, grape, Sun Gold, or baby heirloom)
3 tablespoons olive oil
Kosher salt and cracked black pepper
1 pound angel hair pasta ★
2 medium cloves garlic, minced

1 medium shallot, minced
½ teaspoon red pepper flakes
½ cup white wine
½ cup grated parmesan cheese
4 ounces goat cheese, crumbled
½ cup packed fresh basil leaves

Preheat the oven to 425°F.

On a rimmed baking sheet, toss the tomatoes with 1 tablespoon of the olive oil and season generously with salt and pepper. Roast until the tomatoes darken and begin to burst, 15 to 20 minutes.

Bring a large pot of salted water to a boil. Add the angel hair and cook according to the package directions until al dente. Reserve ½ cup of the starchy cooking water and then drain the pasta. Return the pot to the heat and reduce the heat to medium.

At my family's favorite local Italian spot in Raleigh, I once ordered their phenomenal penne alla vodka with angel hair instead of the traditional tubular pasta. The decadent sauce clung to the threadlike strands like they were meant to be together all along. This pasta dish—with its rosy hue, loads of fresh basil, and creamy goat cheese—is my quick-fix adaptation of those rich, memorable flavors.

In the pot, heat the remaining 2 tablespoons olive oil. Add the garlic, shallots, and pepper flakes and season with salt and pepper. Cook, stirring occasionally, until the shallots are translucent, about 2 minutes. Add the white wine and scrape up any browned bits from the bottom. Add the tomatoes and all of their juices and increase the heat to medium-high. Cook for 1 minute and then add the pasta and ¼ cup of the reserved pasta water and toss to combine. Stir in the parmesan and goat cheese and tear in half the basil leaves. If the sauce is too thick, thin it out with a bit more pasta water.

Just before serving, season to taste with salt. Divide among four plates and garnish with the remaining basil (gently torn) and cracked black pepper.

Fanfare Tip

No goat in your cheese drawer? ('Cause really, how could he fit in there?) Here are three substitutes that will still lead you to a creamy creation: cream cheese, mascarpone, or ricotta.

Butternut Squash Tacos with Apple-Fennel Slaw

Don't get me wrong—I'm a carnivore. But occasionally I like to vacation in the vegetarian world and see what I can come up with. If meatless Mexican fare solely consisted of onions, peppers, and orange-colored cheese, taco night would be a sad, sad place. So in this tortilla-wrapped expedition, I explore the world of texture. Sweet butternut squash pairs with crisp, tangy slaw and crumbly, nutty Manchego cheese. Topped with pumpkin seeds for crunch, these are unlike any tacos you've ever experienced.

You can thank me with tequila.

1 medium butternut squash (about 1½ pounds), peeled, seeded, and cut into 1-inch cubes
2 tablespoons olive oil
2 tablespoons honey
Kosher salt and coarse black pepper
½ cup plain Greek yogurt
¼ cup mayonnaise
2 tablespoons apple cider vinegar
½ teaspoon grated orange zest
1 tablespoon fresh orange juice

2 tart apples, such as Pink Lady, cut into matchsticks
1 large fennel bulb, thinly sliced crosswise to make strips (about 2 cups)
2 tablespoons chopped fresh mint
1 cup salted roasted pumpkin seeds, for garnish
12 to 14 small (6-inch) flour tortillas, warmed just before serving
2 cups shredded Manchego or Asiago cheese

Preheat the oven to 425°F.

Fanfare Tip

For an excuse to liven up the first day of the workweek, throw a Meatless Monday party, break out the mini bowls, and let your guests help themselves. Set up an assembly line of the ingredients so everyone can craft their own tacos. Add your personal panache to this lineup with your favorites. Sliced avocados? Caramelized onions? Don't forget the hot sauce.

Toss the squash cubes with the olive oil, 1 tablespoon of the honey, 1 teaspoon salt, and ½ teaspoon pepper and evenly spread them onto a baking sheet. Roast, tossing once halfway through, until the squash is lightly golden brown and tender, 20 to 25 minutes. While the squash is still warm, taste for additional salt, if needed.

In a small bowl, whisk together the yogurt, mayonnaise, vinegar, orange zest, orange juice, the remaining 1 tablespoon honey, and a pinch each of salt and pepper.

In a large bowl, combine the apples, fennel slices, and mint. A few tablespoons at a time, toss the slaw with the dressing until it's coated but not overly saturated. Season to taste with salt and pepper.

In a dry small skillet, toast the pumpkin seeds over medium-low heat, tossing frequently, until lightly golden and very fragrant, about 5 minutes. Immediately remove the seeds from the pan and transfer to a bowl to stop the cooking process.

To assemble the tacos, top each warm tortilla with a scoop of butternut squash, a handful of Manchego, and a dollop of slaw. Garnish each taco with pumpkin seeds.

Rice Noodles with Citrus Peanut Sauce

SERVES 4

We all love takeout, but let's face it: Laziness can get expensive. Turn your very own kitchen into the local Thai bistro with just a few exotic ingredients. Tender rice noodles and bok choy are doused in a nutty, lime-infused sauce and sprinkled with crunchy homemade honey-roasted sunflower seeds.

Can't get that at the Asian café around the corner, can ya?

1 tablespoon unsalted butter, melted
2 teaspoons honey ★
¼ cup unsalted raw sunflower seeds
Kosher salt and coarse black pepper
8 ounces rice noodles ★
4 small heads baby bok choy, stalks and
    leaves separated
1 tablespoon toasted sesame oil
1 tablespoon minced fresh ginger

2 medium cloves garlic, minced
⅓ cup creamy peanut butter ★
¼ cup rice vinegar
¼ cup lower-sodium soy sauce
2 teaspoons fish sauce
2 teaspoons grated lime zest
Juice of 3 limes
½ cup roughly chopped fresh cilantro
¼ cup thinly sliced scallions, for garnish

Preheat the oven to 300°F.

In a small bowl, whisk together the melted butter, honey, and sunflower seeds. Evenly spread the coated seeds on a nonstick baking sheet and roast, stirring once halfway through, until lightly golden brown, 10 to 12 minutes. While they're still hot, sprinkle the seeds generously with salt. Allow them to cool before breaking them apart.

Prepare the rice noodles according to the package directions. Reserve ½ cup of the starchy cooking water, drain the noodles, and rinse them under cool water.

Cut the stalks of the bok choy into ½-inch-thick pieces and roughly chop the leaves.

For me, the most intriguing part about cooking is reimagining flavors that have stuck with me from childhood. One of the stickiest, pun intended, memories was my absolute favorite summertime snack: a rice cake slathered with creamy peanut butter and syrupy honey. This dish is my unique way of retangling those ingredients in a wildly different way.

In the same pot used to cook the noodles, heat the sesame oil over medium heat. Add the ginger, garlic, and bok choy stalks and season with a pinch each of salt and pepper. Cook until very fragrant, 2 to 3 minutes. In a separate small pot over low heat, add the peanut butter, rice vinegar, soy sauce, fish sauce, lime zest, and lime juice and whisk to combine. Simmer until the sauce comes together, about 2 more minutes. If the sauce is too thick, add the pasta water a tablespoon at a time to thin it out. Season to taste with salt and pepper.

Add the rice noodles, cilantro, and bok choy leaves to the pot with the bok choy stems. Add the peanut sauce and toss until well combined. Divide among 4 plates. Garnish with the honey-roasted sunflower seeds and scallions.

Fanfare Tip

No rice noodles nearby? Swap in linguine or angel hair. Need a little more protein? Top these noodles with shrimp, chicken, or, if you're feeling fancy, seared scallops.

Ziti for Bea

In a galaxy far, far away (well, Summit, New Jersey), there exists an enchanting eatery by the name of Marco Polo. This Italian restaurant has fed generations of Slaters for nearly half a century. As my dad was the only one of his siblings to leave Jersey, our family's meals at Marco Polo were rare and treasured occasions, when we would return from our home in North Carolina with our fettuccine flags raised high. I soaked in every bite and fused every memory onto an imaginary scrapbook page. I can recall parmesans and piccatas and pizzas of all kinds.

I remember being fourteen and confidently ordering a Shirley Temple, thinking I had tricked the waiter into serving me alcohol. "Neat, please," I emphasized while adjusting my skort. My dad stink-eyed me from across the table and then lovingly asked if I wanted to split the Caesar. I may have had Raisinets for brains but I was still the baby. I remember watching my sister swipe countless pieces of crusty ciabatta through glossy plates of fruity olive oil. I remember stealing bites of my mom's light-as-air eggplant parmesan, oozing with velvety cheese and dressed in red. I remember laughing along to the playful banter of my grandfather and aunt as they sipped wine and slurped down spaghetti.

But most of all, I remember that there would always, always be ziti for Bea.

For years I witnessed my grandma Bea faithfully order the same dish, the same way. Bea Bea (as we call her) would lightly pat the marinara-stained sleeve of the server. "I'll have the ziti," she would say assuredly. "And you tell them, I want it *in the tin*."

Desperate to come full circle in my story, I called Bea Bea to unload my curiosity about the mysterious metal tin. She was, of all places, sitting in a booth at Marco Polo. I learned that in June of 1972 at her very first dinner at this be-

Bea Bea preparing for her ziti at Marco Polo on June 16, 2009. It was her and my grandfather's sixty-first anniversary.

loved bistro, she had ordered the baked ziti. It had arrived at the table in a metal tin. Not only did this silver dish keep the pasta piping hot, but it became a symbol of nostalgia. For the next several decades, the outside world would change. Loved ones would pass. Familiar places would come and go. But inside the garlic-scented walls of Marco Polo, there would always, always be ziti for Bea.

★ **Crispy Baked Chicken Parmesan with Fresh Mozzarella** (page 118): As a hearty twist on my parents' favorite parm, I swap out the fresh eggplant and sub in chicken coated with an airy, golden crust of Japanese-style breadcrumbs and drape it with luscious fresh mozzarella.

★ **Garlic and Herb—Infused Dipping Oil** (page 105): For a heavenly dipping sauce, I bathe whole garlic cloves and a variety of herbs and spices in buttery extra-virgin olive oil.

Crispy Baked Chicken Parmesan with Fresh Mozzarella

This recipe creates the perfect opportunity to trick your family into eating whole wheat. *Shhh, I won't tell if you don't.* They'll be so distracted by the crunchy herbed chicken and stringy cheese that the pasta they're swirling onto their forks will be a marinara-doused afterthought. I've swapped the traditional breadcrumbs for light, crispy panko—and a quick sear in the pan leaves this chicken with a marvelously golden crust. It comes to a juicy finish in the oven alongside moist, buttery slices of fresh mozzarella.

7½ cups Basil Marinara (page 227)
1 cup panko breadcrumbs
¼ cup grated parmesan cheese
1 tablespoon chopped fresh oregano or
    1 teaspoon dried
1 tablespoon chopped fresh thyme
1 tablespoon chopped fresh parsley
2 teaspoons kosher salt
1 teaspoon coarse black pepper
2 large eggs, beaten
About 1 cup neutral oil (such as vegetable,
    grapeseed, or sunflower), for sautéing

2 pounds chicken breast cutlets (see
    Fanfare Tip)
8 ounces fresh mozzarella cheese, sliced
    into equal rounds
1 pound whole wheat thin spaghetti

GARNISH
½ cup grated parmesan cheese
½ cup packed fresh basil leaves

Make the Basil Marinara and set aside, covered, over low heat.

Preheat the oven to 350°F.

Bring a large pot of salted water to a boil.

In a shallow bowl, combine the panko, parmesan, oregano, thyme, parsley, salt, and pepper. Set up an assembly line starting with a bowl with the beaten eggs, then the breadcrumb mixture, and a clean plate on the end.

In a large skillet, heat 2 tablespoons of the neutral oil over medium-high heat. Dip a chicken breast into the eggs and then press into the breadcrumbs, shaking off any excess. Place the breaded chicken pieces into the pan, 3 to 4 at a time, and sauté until golden brown, 1 to 2 minutes per side, adding more oil as needed. Transfer the cooked chicken to the clean plate while you finish cooking the rest.

In a shallow 2-quart baking dish, evenly layer the chicken, mozzarella, and several spoonfuls of the marinara. Bake until the chicken is fully cooked through and the cheese has melted, 10 to 15 minutes.

While the chicken is baking, add the thin spaghetti to the boiling water and cook according to the package directions until al dente. Drain the pasta and toss with the remaining marinara.

Divide the pasta evenly among dinner plates. Top the pasta with the baked chicken. Garnish with the parmesan and tear the fresh basil leaves over the top of each plate.

Fanfare Tips

- Since red sauce and red wine are a match made in heaven, you can't go wrong. But if you're really looking to please your palate, pair this satisfying chicken parmigiana with a full-bodied California Cab featuring dark fruity flavors and savory notes of black pepper.
- Can't find those convenient, already-thin chicken cutlets at your local market? Bring home regular boneless, skinless breasts and lay them flat on your cutting board. One at a time, place your palm on top of the chicken and, with a very sharp knife parallel to the board, slice horizontally through the center of the breast to create two thin pieces. Congratulations, you just made cutlets!

Saturday Grilled Chicken with Whiskey BBQ Sauce and Caramelized Pineapple

SERVES 4

Whiskey. Saturday. Chicken.

Some things just belong together.

Next time you're invited to that Saturday barbecue and you're forced to decide between bringing food or booze, be the hero that brings both—in one dish. Barbecue sauces can be made with a thousand different ingredient tweaks. I like mine rich, smoky, savory, sweet, tangy, and acidic all in one. Oh yeah, and whiskey-flavored. If it's not cookout season, finish these flavorful marinated thighs on a grill pan. If it's currently flip-flop weather, we'll cross the finish line on the outdoor grill. Serve up the extra sauce for dipping.

12 bone-in, skin-on chicken thighs (about 3 pounds)
Kosher salt and coarse black pepper
2 tablespoons chopped fresh rosemary
Whiskey BBQ Sauce (recipe follows)

1 tablespoon olive oil
1 tablespoon honey
½ pineapple, peeled, cored, and cut into ½-inch-thick rings
Juice of ½ lime

Generously season the chicken thighs with salt, pepper, and the rosemary and place in a large bowl. Pour half of the Whiskey BBQ Sauce over the chicken, cover, refrigerate, and marinate for at least 1 hour and preferably 3 hours. Let the chicken sit at room temperature for 20 minutes before cooking.

Preheat the oven to 350°F.

Arrange the marinated chicken pieces in a single layer in a 9 x 13-inch baking dish and roast for 1 hour and 15 minutes. Insert a thermometer into the thickest piece and make sure it reaches an internal temperature of 165°F.

Preheat a grill or grill pan to medium-high.

Arrange the chicken thighs on the grill and baste with more Whiskey BBQ Sauce. Cook untouched for 5 minutes, flip each piece, baste again with sauce, and cook for 5 more minutes. The thighs should be lightly charred and slathered in sauce.

In a small bowl, whisk together the olive oil and honey and brush onto both sides of the pineapple rings. Grill until caramelized, 2 to 3 minutes per side. Sprinkle the grilled pineapple with kosher salt and lime juice and serve alongside the chicken.

Whiskey BBQ Sauce

MAKES 2½ CUPS

2 tablespoons olive oil
1 small shallot, minced
½ small sweet onion, minced
2 medium cloves garlic, minced
Kosher salt and coarse black pepper
2 tablespoons tomato paste
½ cup sweet Irish whiskey, such as
    Jameson

1 cup ketchup
¼ cup apple cider vinegar
2 tablespoons Worcestershire sauce
2 tablespoons water
1 teaspoon liquid smoke
2 tablespoons dark brown sugar
1 tablespoon yellow mustard

In a large saucepan, heat the olive oil over medium heat. Add the shallot, onion, and garlic, season with a pinch each of salt and pepper, and cook until translucent, 3 to 5 minutes. Add the tomato paste, whisk to combine, and cook for 1 minute. Add the whiskey and scrape up any browned bits from the bottom. Add the ketchup, vinegar, Worcestershire, water, liquid smoke, brown sugar, and mustard. Stir well to combine and reduce the heat to low.

Using an immersion blender (or transferring the sauce to a stand blender), pulse until smooth. Simmer on low, stirring occasionally, for at least 30 minutes and preferably for 1 hour (which will make the flavors even richer). Season to taste with salt and pepper.

Flippidy-Doo

This versatile boozy barbecue sauce isn't just for basting onto juicy thighs. Here are three other uses: Toss with pulled rotisserie chicken meat for tangy quesadillas, douse baked ribs for a finger-licking appetizer, or spread onto yeasty dough for a smoky base for homemade pizza.

Pulled Buffalo Chicken Tacos with Red Onions and Poblanos

What is it about Buffalo sauce that we all love so much? I'm going to let you in on the secret. Come close. B-u-t-t-e-r. Yep, that creaminess that softens up the spice and melts in your mouth is *butter*—the base of all that is good and holy hot. Toss this easy homemade sauce with roasted pulled chicken thighs and veggies for a taco bar that brings the heat.

Cervezas not included.

2 pounds boneless, skinless chicken thighs
Kosher salt and coarse black pepper
1 tablespoon paprika
2 tablespoons neutral oil (such as vegetable, grapeseed, or sunflower)
2 poblano peppers, seeded and cut into strips
1 small red onion, sliced
2 teaspoons chili powder

¼ cup white wine or chicken stock
Homemade Buffalo Sauce (recipe follows)
12 to 14 small (6-inch) flour tortillas, warmed just before serving
2 cups shredded Monterey Jack cheese
2 cups chopped romaine lettuce
1 small bunch cilantro, roughly chopped, for garnish
Lime wedges, for garnish

Preheat the oven to 350°F.

Generously season both sides of the chicken thighs with salt, pepper, and the paprika.

In a large skillet, heat the oil over medium-high heat. Add the chicken thighs and sear until golden brown, 2 to 3 minutes per side. Arrange the chicken in a single layer in a 9 x 13-inch baking dish.

To the same skillet, add the poblanos and red onion and reduce the heat to medium. Season with the chili powder and a pinch each of salt and pepper and cook until the onions are translucent, about 2 minutes. Add the wine or stock and cook for an additional minute, scraping up the browned bits from the bottom of the pan.

Transfer the veggies and liquid to the baking dish with the chicken and bake for 40 minutes. Remove the chicken from the oven and use two forks to shred the meat. Return the shredded meat to the baking dish, toss it with all of the dish's juices, and bake for an additional 15 minutes.

Drain the majority of the cooking liquid from the baking dish and then toss the chicken and veggies with the Buffalo sauce.

To assemble the tacos, top each warm tortilla with a scoop of the Buffalo chicken, shredded cheese, and lettuce. Garnish each taco with cilantro and a lime wedge.

Homemade Buffalo Sauce

MAKES 1½ CUPS

6 tablespoons (¾ stick) unsalted butter
1 small clove garlic, minced
1 cup Louisiana-style hot sauce (your favorite brand)

1 tablespoon lemon juice
Kosher salt

In a small saucepan, melt the butter over medium-low heat. Add the garlic and cook for 2 minutes. Add the hot sauce and lemon juice and whisk to combine. Simmer for 5 minutes and then season to taste with salt.

Fanfare Tip

Love the buttery Buffalo spice but not the Buffalo? You know what I mean. Swap out the pulled chicken for some veggies—eggplant, zucchini, and squash do an excellent job of absorbing the sauce.

Flippidy-Doo

Try topping these sassy vegetarian tacos with Lime Poppy Seed Slaw (page 163) for a refreshing citrusy crunch.

Madeira Chicken with Tarragon and Shiitakes

Welcome to your new favorite weeknight dinner. In this artfully simplistic dish, chicken thighs and breasts are paired with earthy mushrooms and immersed in a rich blend of smooth, nutty Madeira wine and anise-scented tarragon. The bone-in pieces stay wildly moist and tender, and a touch of orange zest at the end creates a surprising burst of citrusy freshness.

2 tablespoons neutral oil (such as vegetable, grapeseed, or sunflower)

1½ pounds bone-in, skin-on chicken thighs

1½ pounds bone-in, skin-on chicken breast halves

Kosher salt and coarse black pepper

1 tablespoon unsalted butter

1 medium shallot, sliced

2 small fennel bulbs, cut into ½-inch-thick wedges (reserve and chop some of the fennel fronds for garnish)

2 medium cloves garlic, minced

1 cup sliced shiitake mushroom caps (about 3 ounces)

½ cup Madeira wine

1 cup lower-sodium chicken stock

GARNISH

1 tablespoon roughly chopped fresh tarragon

½ teaspoon grated orange zest

Fanfare Tips

- No Madeira on hand? Pour in that leftover white wine taking up space in your fridge. To pour in your glass: a light, minerally unoaked Chardonnay.
- For a true one-pot meal, throw 2 pounds small Yukon Golds into the mix. Halve the potatoes and add them to the pan along with the shallots and fennel. Crank up the salt and pepper a bit on this layer as potatoes require a heavier hand for seasoning.

Preheat the oven to 400°F. In a large cast-iron skillet, heat the oil over medium-high heat. Generously season the chicken pieces with salt and pepper on both sides. Working in batches so you don't overcrowd, sear each piece about 2 minutes per side, and then set aside on a plate.

Reduce the heat to medium and add the butter. Add the shallots and fennel, season with salt and pepper, and cook until translucent, about 5 minutes. Add the garlic and shiitakes and cook until the mushrooms are browned, about 5 more minutes.

Add the Madeira to the pan and scrape any browned bits from the bottom. Add the chicken stock and simmer for 5 minutes. Return the chicken pieces and all of their juices to the pan. Place the entire pan, uncovered, in the oven and bake until the chicken is cooked through, 35 to 40 minutes.

Remove the chicken pieces from the pan and arrange them on a platter. Season the sauce to taste with salt and pepper and then pour it over the sauce over the chicken. Garnish with the chopped fennel fronds, chopped tarragon, and orange zest.

Touched by Chicken

My life has been touched by chicken.

Don't worry, I washed my hands afterward.

For me, walking through my parents' mahogany-glazed front door and in-stantaneously being embraced by the warm aroma of nutty roasted garlic and woody rosemary is the quintessence of home.

In the land of epic roast chicken, my dad is the mayor, the president, and the duke of dark meat. In what felt like the blink of an eye, he would transform a gangly whole fowl into an elegant meal of golden chicken pieces surrounded by delicate vegetables. I studied his every move as he would toss a kitchen towel over his left shoulder, drain the Pinot from his glass, and scatter finely chopped herbs over our finished plates. It was like watching a trapeze artist in the circus steadily walk a straight line and finish by gracefully swinging himself on top of a giraffe.

I felt out of place in traditional school but found myself to be an overachiever in this home-taught chicken course. My dad's go-to poultry methods were roast-ing and grilling. On a typical night, he would gently brush the chicken's bumpy skin with grassy olive oil and sharp, pungent crushed garlic. A parade of paprika and then into the oven the bird would go. When the warm weather surfaced, I would find him standing on our deck inside a hazy cloud of lemon-scented smoke—pot holder on one hand and tuna-smeared cracker in the other. It was under his tutelage that I discovered sophisticated snacking was a vital step in mealtime preparation.

In order to replicate the crispy exterior my dad's chicken was never without, today I pan-sear each piece. Not only does this produce a flavorful crust on the skin, it locks in the meat's juices and seasons the pan for the next round of in-gredients. When it's grill season, I break out the whiskey (see Saturday Grilled

Dad and his beloved aunt Annette—who introduced him to the world of Julia Child—smoking lemony chicken over charcoal.

Chicken with Whiskey BBQ Sauce and Caramelized Pineapple: page 120), begin at the oven, and finish strong with char marks. I use these techniques not only to craft a beautifully browned bird, but also to fill my present kitchen with the comforting smells of past chicken celebrations.

* **Madeira Chicken with Tarragon and Shiitakes** (page 124): In this dish I take advantage of the savory, caramelized bits the seared chicken leaves behind and deglaze with a nutty fortified wine to create a rich pan sauce.

* **Saturday Grilled Chicken with Whiskey BBQ Sauce and Caramelized Pineapple** (page 120): This dish is an ode to cherished charcoal memories with my dad. I slather juicy roasted thighs in a sweet, homemade barbecue sauce with a kick of booze and fire up the grill for the finale.

Sweet Onion Potato Chip–Crusted Chicken with Maple Honey Mustard

SERVES 4

You know that desperate moment when you're caught hands-deep in an empty bag of potato chips licking the bottom-crumbs from between your fingers? This is a recipe that not only redeems but embraces that awkward situation. Juicy baked chicken breasts are covered in a crisp oniony coating of chips and dressed with a peppery, tangy maple drizzle. Serve with a fresh, citrusy green salad.

1 bag (5 ounces) onion-flavored kettle-cooked potato chips

2 large eggs

1 tablespoon Dijon mustard

1 tablespoon half-and-half

Kosher salt and coarse black pepper

4 boneless, skinless chicken breast halves (6 ounces each)

¼ cup olive oil

1 tablespoon paprika

Maple Honey Mustard (recipe follows)

Preheat the oven to 350°F. Grease a baking sheet.

Put the potato chips in a Ziploc bag, squeeze the air out, and seal. Wrap the plastic bag in a kitchen towel and, using a rolling pin or potato masher, crush the chips into fine crumbs. Place the crumbs in a large shallow bowl.

In a separate shallow bowl, whisk together the eggs, mustard, and half-and-half and generously season with salt and pepper. Lay out an assembly line of the chicken, egg mixture, and potato chips. Have the greased baking sheet ready at the end.

Fanfare Tips

- Round up the youngsters for the chip-crushing portion of this recipe. They'll have a blast crunching up the coating and feel like an important behind-the-scenes member of this meal. Take it one step further by bringing them to the grocery store to pick out their favorite chip flavor.

- For a sweet and smoky coated chicken, snatch up your favorite brand of barbecue chips. For a tangy twist, salt and vinegar will do the trick.

Dip one chicken breast into the egg mixture and then coat in the crushed potato chips, pressing to help them adhere. Transfer the chicken to the baking sheet and repeat until all the chicken pieces are fully crusted with the chips. Evenly drizzle both sides of the chicken pieces with the oil and season both sides with salt, pepper, and the paprika. ★

Bake the chicken until the outside crust is golden brown and the center of the largest piece is no longer pink, 20 to 25 minutes. While the chicken breasts are still hot, sprinkle them with salt.

Drizzle each breast with 2 tablespoons of the Maple Honey Mustard.

Maple Honey Mustard

MAKES ½ CUP

¼ cup Dijon mustard
1 tablespoon mayonnaise
1 teaspoon honey

2 tablespoons maple syrup
1 teaspoon Worcestershire sauce
Kosher salt and coarse black pepper

In a small bowl, whisk together the mustard, mayonnaise, honey, maple syrup, and Worcestershire and season to taste with salt and pepper. The flavor should be heavy on the black pepper.

★ Before I could even see over the kitchen counter, my dad schooled me on the art of homemade eats. Standing on a chair by his side, I remember watching him dredge and coat pale, pink chicken strips in an assembly line of ingredients. That night I had requested chicken fingers, and frozen, bagged, and thawed were out of the question. He was determined to teach me to cook from scratch, and it was through these crusty tenders he tutored me on seasoned breadcrumbs for crunch and paprika for warmth and color. This was the kind of class where I paid attention.

Deep-Fried Tradition

I was blessed with a big sister who brushed out my tangles, laughed at my jokes, and didn't even mind when I would frolick around with her bra on my head.

I remember the first time she asked me to make her breakfast, and how I put my heart and soul into it. At age eight, my five-star creation was cheese toast. But to Sarah, it was the *best cheese toast she had ever tasted* as she—like my parents—celebrated and adored everything I did. In 2004, Sarah became enchanted by Hawaii, and the tropical paradise has been her home ever since. I couldn't imagine not having her at arm's reach, but that sacrifice laid the foundation for a future of exotic edible experiences for our whole family.

Once a year, my mom, dad, and I soar across the map to Sarah's island abode, where the four of us spend two weeks back under the same roof. On one

Dad and Sarah documenting our annual sushi spree with a deep-fried selfie.

of our first trips, she led us straight to Sansei—a modern sushi eatery with inventive Japanese twists.

They were famous for one sushi dish in particular, the panko-crusted ahi. The dish arrived at the table for us to share; it was a narrow barrel shape surrounded by a chestnut-colored sauce. This "sushi" seemed to be in disguise. As it turned out, this mysterious log was made up of slices of rosy tuna enclosed in a golden, flash-fried panko shell. With a nudge of my finger, I toppled the end slice to reveal its extraordinary pink core to the world. Somewhere, an angel cried. (Or maybe it was a baby in the restaurant. I'm not sure. I was pretty focused on the ahi.) I dragged the magnificent morsel through its decadent pool of butter, soy, and wasabi and popped the entire thing into my mouth. It was light, silky, and peppery, and the lush sauce melted like velvet onto my tongue.

We ordered two more.

What had begun as a standard seafood dinner ended as the origin of future ceremonial feasts, a ritual for each of our subsequent stays on Oahu. The panko-crusted ahi has become as valuable to our Hawaiian vacation as the sunscreen my dad smears onto his fair-skinned toes. As I re-create these flavors at home on the mainland, not only am I summoning a memento from my family's annual two weeks under the sun, I'm capturing our deep-fried tradition in my very own kitchen.

★ **Seared Tuna with Spicy Guava Butter and Crushed Macadamias** (page 132): Deeply inspired by Sansei's flavors, I set out to create a creamy mixture of my own to pair with quick-seared fish. I whisk velvety butter into thick, fruity reduced guava juice for a sweet, silky sauce to coat ever-so-slightly-cooked tuna. To mimic the crunch of the crispy fried panko shell, I crush macadamia nuts over top.

Seared Tuna with Spicy Guava Butter and Crushed Macadamias

SERVES 4

Remember the three things you chose when someone asked what you would bring to a desert island? One of them is about to get bumped for this dish. With rich, exotically flavored guava nectar as a base to create a sweet buttery sauce for rare tuna, this fish will whisk you straight to a tropical island. If you're already stranded in paradise . . . don't forget your fork.

½ cup Spicy Guava Butter (page 226)
¼ cup roughly chopped macadamia nuts, for garnish
4 thick, sushi-grade tuna steaks (6 ounces each)

Kosher salt and coarse black pepper
2 tablespoons neutral oil (such as vegetable, grapeseed, or sunflower)
1 tablespoon chopped fresh dill, for garnish

Make the guava butter and keep at room temperature.

In a dry small skillet, toast the macadamia nuts over medium-low heat, tossing frequently, until lightly golden and very fragrant, about 5 minutes. Immediately remove the nuts from the pan and transfer to a bowl to stop the cooking process.

Season each tuna steak generously with salt and pepper on each side.

In a large skillet, heat the oil over high heat. Carefully lay the tuna steaks in the pan (do this in batches if your skillet is not big enough) and sear each piece 1 to 2 minutes per side, depending on their thickness.

Thinly slice each steak on an angle. Evenly distribute the Spicy Guava Butter among 4 plates and fan out the tuna slices on top. Garnish with the macadamia nuts and dill.

Fanfare Tip

To accompany the sweet notes of the guava butter, look for a floral Riesling or a fruity, melon-scented rosé. Search for a dry variety of either wine—as the flavor will be a more complex complement to the dish.

Marinated Lamb with Rosemary Roasted Scallion Pesto

SERVES 4

Lamb is beef's rowdy next-door neighbor. It's b-a-a-a-d to the bone. Or boneless, in this case. Lamb is succulent, juicy, and rich in meat flavor. In this play on the classic combination of lamb and rosemary, a tender, marinated boneless leg of lamb is finished with a fresh roasted scallion pesto made with sunflower seeds and laced with lemon.

⅓ cup olive oil
2 small cloves garlic, minced
3 tablespoons fresh lemon juice
2 teaspoons dried oregano
½ teaspoon ground cumin
1 teaspoon kosher salt

½ teaspoon coarse black pepper
1½ pounds boneless lamb ★ leg, cut into
    4 thick fillets
½ cup Rosemary Roasted Scallion Pesto
    (page 213)

In a small bowl, whisk together the olive oil, garlic, lemon juice, oregano, cumin, salt, and pepper. Place the lamb in a large bowl, pour the marinade over the fillets, toss to combine, cover, and refrigerate for at least 3 hours. Take the lamb out of the fridge 20 minutes before cooking.

Heat a dry large skillet over medium-high heat. Shake the excess marinade off the lamb and carefully drop into the pan. Sear the lamb for 3 minutes on the first side and 2 minutes on the second. Reduce the heat to low, cover the pan with a lid, and cook for 1 additional minute for medium-rare. Remove the lamb from the heat and allow it to rest for 5 minutes.

Thinly slice each lamb fillet against the grain and top with the pesto.

Flippidy-Doo

Turn this indoor entrée into an outdoor app by thinly slicing the lamb and skewering it over the grill with some veggies. Brush with the pesto and serve alongside Rustic Panzanella with Olive Vinaigrette (page 167).

★ Being the only lamb-consuming member of my family, as a kid I would patiently watch my dad preparing my personal meal. He would sprinkle bright green rosemary and slather smashed garlic over the meat, and then under the broiler the savory chops would go, humming with earthy herbs and oniony aromas. This is my reinvention of those glorious flavors.

Moroccan-Spiced Turkey Meatballs with Coconut Basil Marinara

Cloudy with a chance of . . . cinnamon? That's right. From the outside this dish appears to be an Italian classic, but one bite will travel your taste buds to Morocco. Enhanced with warm spices like cumin and coriander, these light meatballs are a flavor vacation. The key to keeping them moist: a quick sear on the outside and then into the coconut marinara for a swim to the finish line.

COCONUT MARINARA

½ recipe Basil Marinara (page 227)
1 cup canned unsweetened coconut milk

MEATBALLS

1 tablespoon olive oil
1 medium shallot, minced
2 medium cloves garlic, minced
Kosher salt and coarse black pepper
1 pound ground turkey
1 large egg, beaten
½ cup fine dried breadcrumbs
1 tablespoon chopped fresh mint

1 tablespoon chopped fresh cilantro
1 teaspoon ground coriander
1 teaspoon ground cumin ★
1 teaspoon paprika
¼ teaspoon ground cinnamon
About 4 tablespoons neutral oil (such as vegetable, grapeseed, or sunflower), for searing

GARNISH

½ cup crumbled feta cheese
1 tablespoon chopped fresh cilantro

Make the coconut marinara: In a wide saucepan, make the basil marinara as directed and simmer for 30 minutes. Whisk in the coconut milk, cover, and keep on low heat while you prepare the rest of the ingredients. (The torn basil for the marinara gets added later, when you put the meatballs in the sauce.)

On our annual Hawaiian trip to visit my sister, my family has a dependable collection of restaurant staples. One year, Sarah convinced us that Casablanca was an essential addition to our list—and she was right. This Moroccan-style restaurant was a graceful palace of exotic eating, where the floor was your seat and the flavors were intoxicating. It was my first dance with warm, peppery cumin . . . and I let him lead.

Make the meatballs: In a small skillet, heat the olive oil over medium heat. Add the shallot and garlic, season with a pinch of salt and pepper, and cook until translucent, 2 to 3 minutes. Transfer to a large bowl to cool to room temperature.

To the cooled shallot mixture, add the turkey, egg, breadcrumbs, mint, cilantro, coriander, cumin, paprika, cinnamon, 1 teaspoon salt, and ½ teaspoon pepper. Gently fold the mixture together. Using a ¼-cup scoop, form the mixture into 10 to 12 equal-size meatballs.

In a large nonstick skillet, heat 2 tablespoons of the neutral oil over medium-high heat. Add as many meatballs as you can without crowding the pan. Working in batches, sear the sides of the meatballs until a golden brown crust forms all over, 30 to 45 seconds per side. Add more oil to each batch as needed.

Stir the torn basil from the marinara recipe into the coconut marinara. Place the browned meatballs in the marinara and cover with sauce so they are completely immersed. Cover the pot and simmer over low heat until the meatballs are cooked through, 15 to 20 minutes.

Garnish with crumbled feta and cilantro.

Fanfare Tip

Serve these unique meatballs with a simple green salad and crunchy herbed garlic bread to sop up all the exotic sauce. For the wine, a slightly chilled Côtes du Rhône will complement the spices and refresh your palate.

Homemade FAN Macs with Garlicky Dill Pickles

MAKES 4 BURGERS

There are certain fast foods we all crave from time to time. Don't blame yourself; go home and *make them yourself*. Lighten up with juicy pan-seared turkey burgers and *relish* the crunch of homemade pickles. Yeah, I punned. That's what's up.

The sauce makes a few spoonfuls more than you'll need, but you'll want to dip your homemade steak fries, chips, or fingers in it—so go for the full recipe. The homemade pickles take 2 days, so let the games begin or opt for the quick fix from the store.

1 pound ground turkey
2 tablespoons olive oil
2 tablespoons Worcestershire sauce
2 teaspoons Dijon mustard
½ teaspoon kosher salt
¼ teaspoon coarse black pepper
1 tablespoon unsalted butter, melted

4 slices white American cheese
4 sesame seed buns, split open
FAN Sauce (recipe follows)
½ cup Garlicky Dill Pickles (page 196) or store-bought
1 cup shredded iceberg lettuce

Preheat the oven to 350°F.

In a large bowl, combine the ground turkey, 1 tablespoon of the olive oil, the Worcestershire, mustard, salt, and pepper. Form the meat mixture into 4 equal patties and season the outsides with a pinch of salt and pepper.

In a large nonstick skillet, heat the remaining 1 tablespoon olive oil and ½ tablespoon of the butter over medium-high heat. Add the turkey burgers and sear for 3 minutes on the first side. Reduce the heat to medium, flip the burgers, and cook for 4 minutes on the other side. Then transfer them to a baking sheet. Bake until the patties reach an internal temperature of 165°F, 6 to 8 minutes. They should be tender to the touch and no longer pink on the inside.

Top each patty with a slice of cheese and allow it to melt in the oven, about 1 minute.

In the pan used to cook the burgers, heat the remaining ½ tablespoon butter over medium heat and toast the buns until they are lightly golden brown, 1 to 2 minutes.

To assemble the burgers, spread each toasted bottom bun with some FAN Sauce and then top with a burger patty, pickles, shredded iceberg, one more drizzle of FAN Sauce, and the top bun.

FAN Sauce

MAKES ½ CUP

¼ cup mayonnaise
2 tablespoons ketchup
2 teaspoons finely minced sweet onion
2 teaspoons finely minced homemade or
    store-bought pickles

1 teaspoon pickle juice from the jar
1 teaspoon sugar
Kosher salt and coarse black pepper

In a small bowl, whisk together the mayonnaise, ketchup, onion, pickles, pickle juice, and sugar. Season to taste with salt and pepper.

Flippidy-Doo

Double the FAN Sauce and use it for turkey Reubens this week-end. Fresh sliced rye, turkey piled high, Swiss cheese, extra sauce, and slaw. Or keep it simple by toasting up a grilled cheese with the leftover American singles and FAN sauce.

Pan-Seared Steak with Sage Butter

If you're looking for a high-quality yet inexpensive cut of meat, go no further, my friend. This recipe calls for teres major—also known as shoulder petite tender steak. This variety is wildly wallet-friendly and as tender as can be. The secret? *It's a secret.* No, really. With only two slabs of this cut per cow, most butchers save these gems for themselves. But ask . . . and you shall receive. Topped with earthy sage butter, these steaks just need a quick ride in a cast-iron pan to be seared to perfection.

4 tablespoons (½ stick) unsalted butter, at room temperature
1 tablespoon finely chopped fresh sage
1 teaspoon grated lemon zest
Kosher salt and cracked black pepper

½ tablespoon neutral oil (such as vegetable, grapeseed, or sunflower)
4 shoulder petite tender steaks (aka teres major), about 6 ounces each

In a small bowl, mix together the butter, sage, lemon zest, and a pinch each of salt and pepper. Keep at room temperature.

Allow the steaks to sit at room temperature for 20 minutes before cooking. In a large cast-iron skillet, heat the oil over high heat. Pat each steak dry and season both sides generously with salt and pepper. Add the steaks to the pan and cook, untouched, for 2 minutes on the first side and 1 minute on the second side.

Turn the heat to low and cover the pan for 1 minute. Allow the steaks to sit covered off the heat for 2 minutes.

Divide the steaks among 4 plates and top each one with a spoonful of the sage butter.

Fanfare Tip

If you're in the mood for moo, opt for a shop with a butcher on hand or an expert in the meat department. The packages lining the grocery store aisles aren't your only option. Most meat departments will cut, trim, and tenderize what's in the glass case or even share whatever is handy in the back.

Scallop Piccata with Caramelized Fennel

When I say "piccata," you say "chicken"! Not in this recipe, ya don't. Golden on the outside, silky smooth on the inside, sea scallops are the main attraction in this main course. Partnered with sweet, crunchy caramelized fennel, this is a tangy piccata unlike any other. Serve with crusty ciabatta or your favorite pasta for sauce-sopping.

2½ tablespoons neutral oil (such as vegetable, grapeseed, or sunflower)
16 large sea scallops (about 2 pounds)
Kosher salt and coarse black pepper
2 tablespoons unsalted butter
1 small fennel bulb, thinly sliced (about 1 cup)

1 teaspoon honey
2 medium cloves garlic, minced
½ cup white wine
¼ cup fresh lemon juice
2 tablespoons capers
¼ cup chopped fresh parsley

In a large skillet, heat 2 tablespoons of the neutral oil over medium-high heat. Pat the scallops dry and season both sides with salt and pepper. Sear until golden brown, about 2 minutes per side. Set the scallops aside on a plate.

Reduce the heat to medium-low and add 1 tablespoon of the butter. Add the fennel and honey and sauté until the fennel is lightly golden and caramelized, about 15 minutes. Season with a pinch each of salt and pepper. Set the fennel aside on the same plate as the scallops.

Increase the heat to medium and add the remaining ½ tablespoon oil. Add the garlic and cook until translucent, about 1 minute. Add the white wine and lemon juice and scrape up any browned bits from the bottom of the pan.

Increase the heat to medium-high and cook for 2 minutes to reduce the liquid. Remove the pan from the heat and stir in the remaining 1 tablespoon butter, the capers, and parsley.

Add the caramelized fennel and scallops (with their juices) back to the pan, spooning the warm liquid over them. Divide among 4 plates and serve immediately.

Fanfare Tip

Spice up this scallop entrée by adding angel hair with a kick. Cook the pasta until al dente and then sauté with olive oil, parmesan, and red pepper flakes. Pour the scallops and their sauce over the noodles. Serve with a mineraly California oaked Chardonnay to contrast with the buttery richness of the piccata.

Taco Bar

Dinner at home was like dining at an elegant restaurant . . . in your pajamas. The food was never intricate or fussy, but homemade, soulful spreads were a nightly experience in our house. We feasted on black bean cakes, grilled swordfish, and sublimely roasted Cornish hen. However, there was no meal in our kitchen that my friends looked forward to more than taco night.

My parents would line our oak table with ramekins and pile shredded romaine, chopped cilantro, and sharp cheddar into the multicolored mini bowls. It was my job to dollop the sour cream. I remember toasty tortillas, citrusy grilled chicken, and silky avocado slices my mom would fan out onto a platter. My friends would take turns at the microwave, watching the gooey cheese bubble and spread out over their naked tortillas. Then, with our bare fingers, like tiny chefs at work, we would compose our plates with toppings of all textures and sizes. A pinch of diced tomatoes here, a squeeze of lime there.

In search of inspiration for family taco night, Dad studies the fine art of fresh lime juice, salt, and tequila. He takes this very seriously.

The food was excellent, but it was the interactive experience of building our own dinner that, later down the road, would inspire me to explore all types of taco fillings.

★ **Fish Tacos with Pickled Radishes and Grilled Pineapple Aioli** (page 142): For a handheld summery bite, I top fresh flaky fish with a creamy, smoky pineapple spread and quick pickled radishes.

★ **Butternut Squash Tacos with Apple-Fennel Slaw** (page 112): My taste buds can't help but occasionally tiptoe into the exotic world of gourmet vegetarian cuisine. In these fall-friendly meatless tacos, bright, anise-scented slaw adds a tangy crunch to sweet roasted butternut squash.

★ **Pulled Buffalo Chicken Tacos with Red Onions and Poblanos** (page 122): As a stand-in for traditional grilled chicken breast, I pile tortillas with sweet red onions, smoky poblanos, and tender shredded chicken thighs simmered in a rich, buttery sauce.

Fish Tacos with Pickled Radishes and Grilled Pineapple Aioli

What is it about fish tacos that makes you want to quit your job and become a professional margarita tester? In this recipe, it's the sauce. Juicy grilled lemon and pineapple zip together to create a sweet, roasty aioli that you'll want to drizzle over just about everything. A zesty spice rub gives a kick to mild white fish, buttery avocado adds creaminess, and pickled radishes bring a fresh, vibrant bite.

BYOTequila.

PICKLED RADISHES

1 cup distilled white vinegar

1 cup water

1 tablespoon sugar

1 teaspoon kosher salt

1 bunch radishes, very thinly sliced into rounds

FISH

2 teaspoons paprika

2 teaspoons light brown sugar

1 teaspoon cayenne pepper

1 teaspoon chili powder

1 teaspoon garlic powder

Kosher salt and coarse black pepper

2 pounds flaky white fish fillets (such as cod, tilapia, or mahi)

1 tablespoon neutral oil (such as vegetable, grapeseed, or sunflower)

½ tablespoon unsalted butter

TACOS

3 avocados

1 tablespoon olive oil

Juice of 1 lime

Kosher salt

12 to 14 small (6-inch) flour tortillas, warmed just before serving

2 cups shredded red cabbage

Grilled Pineapple Aioli (page 222)

Make the pickled radishes: In a small saucepan, whisk together the vinegar, water, sugar, and salt and bring to a boil over high heat.

Fanfare Tip

Try the spice rub on shrimp or scallops for another seafood-y spin on the traditional taco.

Place the radishes in a heatproof airtight container. Pour the boiling liquid over the radishes, cover the container with a lid, and let sit at room temperature for at least 30 minutes. If you're making these in advance, refrigerate them until you're ready to use.

Cook the fish: In a small bowl, mix together the paprika, brown sugar, cayenne pepper, chili powder, garlic powder, and 2 teaspoons salt. Season both sides of the fish with salt and black pepper and about half of the spice rub.

In a large nonstick skillet, heat the neutral oil and butter over medium-high heat. Add the fish and sear for 3 minutes on the first side and 2 minutes on the second. If the fillets are very thick, cover the pan with a lid, reduce the heat to low, and cook until the center of the fish is opaque. Remove the pan from the heat, flake the fish into large pieces with a fork, sprinkle with the remaining spice rub, and gently fold with any juices remaining in the pan.

Prepare the tacos: Halve the avocados lengthwise and remove the pit by carefully rapping it with a knife (so the blade wedges into it) and twisting to remove. Discard the pit. Use a spoon to remove the avocado's flesh and cut into chunks.

In a medium bowl, combine the avocado, olive oil, and lime juice and mash the mixture with a fork until it is smooth but chunky. Season to taste with salt.

To assemble the tacos, top each warm tortilla with a spoonful of avocado mash, shredded cabbage, fish, and pickled radishes. Drizzle each taco with the pineapple aioli.

Individual Cheesy Lobster Mac with Caramelized Shallots

It's homemade mac and cheese night and everyone's after the crispy topping. Here's where I come in. Not to steal your topping, just to give you some advice. Although I did travel a long way . . .

Rather than the family-size casserole of this cheesy favorite, I prefer my own personal serving. And I want it with lobster. Opt for your next mac and cheese Fanny-style, where everyone gets a crunchy breadcrumb garnish of their very own. Instead of a traditional béchamel-based sauce, this seafood specialty starts with a light homemade lobster stock.

1 tablespoon unsalted butter

1 small shallot, thinly sliced

Kosher salt and coarse black pepper

½ cup cavatelli pasta

1 lobster tail (4 ounces), raw meat chopped and shell reserved

¼ cup dry white wine

⅓ cup water

1 medium clove garlic, gently smashed but still intact

½ lemon

1 tablespoon mascarpone cheese or cream cheese

Pinch of freshly grated nutmeg

¼ cup grated fontina cheese

¼ cup grated sharp white cheddar cheese

2 teaspoons chopped fresh thyme

1 tablespoon grated parmesan cheese

1 tablespoon panko breadcrumbs

¼ teaspoon paprika

Preheat the oven to 350°F. Grease an ovenproof soup crock or ramekin about 5 inches in diameter.

In a small skillet, heat the butter over low heat. Add the shallot and cook, stirring occasionally, until they are golden and caramelized, 15 to 20 minutes. Season them with a pinch each of salt and pepper.

Fanfare Tips

- For an even richer lobster stock, swap out the white wine for dry sherry.
- A hearty dish like this needs light, fresh greens as the sidecar. Since you'll already be perusing the cheese aisle, go for the Blackberry and Bucheron Salad (page 154).

Meanwhile, bring a large pot of salted water to a boil. Add the cavatelli and cook according to the package directions until al dente. Drain the pasta and set aside.

Meanwhile, in a medium saucepan, combine the lobster shells, white wine, water, and garlic and heat over high heat. Squeeze the lemon into the stock, place the lemon in the pan, and cover. Bring to a boil, reduce the heat to medium, and simmer until the stock is reduced to about ¼ cup, 12 to 15 minutes.

Strain the stock into a large bowl, then whisk in the mascarpone, nutmeg, fontina, cheddar, and ¼ teaspoon each salt and pepper.

To the bowl with the cheese sauce, gently fold in the caramelized shallot, cooked pasta, lobster chunks, and thyme. Spoon the mixture into the greased crock. Mix the parmesan, panko, and the paprika and sprinkle over the top of the cheesy mixture.

Bake for 12 minutes and then broil until the top is lightly golden, 1 to 2 minutes. Keep a close eye on the dish while broiling, as the top browns very quickly.

Spicy Soba Noodles with Shrimp and Hoisin

Have you ever stared into your takeout containers and wished for more broccoli or spicier shrimp? Well, it's time to take matters into your own pans. Skip the delivery fee and customize your stir-fry from scratch. This dish stars thin buckwheat noodles coated in a fragrant sauce of pungent hoisin, salty soy, and tart lime. Swap the shrimp for chicken or beef, and the broccoli for carrots or peppers. Who's the boss? You are.

(Sorry, Mr. Danza.)

3 ounces soba noodles
1 tablespoon toasted sesame oil
½ pound medium shrimp, shelled and
    deveined
Kosher salt and coarse black pepper
1 tablespoon neutral oil (such as
    vegetable, grapeseed, or sunflower)
1 teaspoon minced fresh ginger
1 medium clove garlic, minced
1 small shallot, thinly sliced
½ cup roughly chopped celery
1 cup roughly chopped broccoli

1 teaspoon red pepper flakes
2 tablespoons hoisin sauce
½ teaspoon fish sauce
1 tablespoon soy sauce
1 tablespoon fresh lime juice
½ teaspoon honey
¼ cup snow peas
¼ cup thinly sliced scallions

GARNISH

2 teaspoons black sesame seeds

Cook the soba noodles according to the package directions. Drain, then rinse under cool water.

Fanfare Tip

For a unique and unusual wine pairing, pour a honeysuckle-scented Viognier to partner this meal. Low in acid and high in alcohol, this exotic grape has a perfume of violet and white pepper, which couples brilliantly with aromatic Asian flavors like ginger and garlic.

In a large skillet, heat the sesame oil over medium heat. Season the shrimp with salt and black pepper, then add them to the pan. Cook the shrimp until pink, 1 to 2 minutes per side, depending on their size. Remove the shrimp from the pan and set aside on a plate.

Add the neutral oil to the pan, then the ginger, garlic, shallot, celery, broccoli, and pepper flakes. Season the veggies with salt and black pepper and cook until tender, about 2 minutes. In a small bowl, whisk together the hoisin, fish sauce, soy sauce, lime juice, and honey, then add it to the pan and toss to coat the veggies.

Add the cooked soba noodles to the pan and toss until they are thoroughly coated, about 1 minute. Return the shrimp to the pan along with the snow peas and scallions and toss to combine. Divide the noodles and shrimp evenly between 2 plates and garnish with the sesame seeds.

Balcony Bouillabaisse

There once was a love story so magical that it required no words. Although . . . no love was exchanged and technically no words were spoken, so it's more like a tale of silence, adolescence, and shrimp.

Let's start from the beginning.

Each summer my family would gather our most necessary belongings—the contents of the fridge, the occasional cat, several bathing suits—and drive east to Wrightsville Beach, North Carolina. A first-floor rental condo at Duneridge was our shoreline home-away-from-home and became the backdrop for many of my favorite childhood memories. There, we would spend two sun-drenched weeks sharing paintbrushes, Scrabble tiles, and enormous seaside dinners made with fresh, citrusy ocean fare. There was meaty triggerfish, firm and sweet and showered with lemon. There were plump local clams, stacked to the ceiling and surrounded by golden pools of melted butter. But of all the meals we shared on our cozy, beach-view balcony, nothing stands as lively and present in my mind today as bouillabaisse.

My dad would prepare this hearty seafood stew while singing opera alongside Luciano Pavarotti recordings. I would linger nearby employing a hot dog as a flute. The rich tomatoey broth overflowing with decadent fresh fish, luscious shrimp, and briny mussels was the epitome of coastal nourishment and instilled in me an appreciation for the *fanfare* of the ocean. While my sister was equally grateful for the bountiful homemade meal, in this specific story, our trip was coming to a close and one youthful stone had been left unturned.

As the claps and clangs of the cleared dishes faded from the balcony, Sarah tightened her scrunchie and sighed at the sight of the vacant neighboring patio—when suddenly, the glass door slid open. Out walked Thomas, a handsome pre–Prince Charming with long, glossy dark hair and striking cheekbones for a thirteen-year-old. My mom called out, "Sar, are you coming in to watch the movie?" Sarah spun

Enjoying an evening meal on our breezy Duneridge balcony circa 1992. It would be on this very same patio two years later that my sister, Sarah, would silently fall in love with the boy next door. By then, in that youthful teenage summer, she would no longer sport cornrows (and my parents would finally discover my severe nearsightedness).

around and exuberantly shook her head. The next several hours unfolded in silence as she and Thomas took turns exchanging shy grins and looking away.

The night ended without a single spoken word, and the next morning, Thomas's family packed up and left for the summer. Ambitious and drunk on young love, Sarah retrieved the contact information for the owner of the adjacent condo, Thomas's grandfather. She poured her teenage heart out into a handwritten letter and mailed it off into the universe. Weeks later, a note arrived at our home back in Raleigh. This man did not, in fact, have a grandson named Thomas—but he *did* wish her the best of luck on her search.

Dear Thomas,

If you have read this story and identified yourself as the strapping young teen who once shared a wordless summer evening with my sister, please make yourself known, as this story could use a happier ending. Or at the very least, thank you for buying this cookbook, and I hope you make this recipe.

★ **Quick Coconut Curry with Clams and Mussels** (page 150): I've plucked bouillabaisse from France and reimagined it through a Thai filter. Keeping its original components—seafood and an aromatic red sauce—I've streamlined it into a speedy red curry swimming with lime and creamy coconut milk.

Quick Coconut Curry with Clams and Mussels

This light, exotic feast comes together faster than you can find your stack of to-go menus. The secret to creating a rich, worthy curry that simmers up in no time? It's all in the red curry paste. If you've never worked with shellfish before, don't worry—clams and mussels come equipped with a built-in timer and pop open when they're ready. I opted for leeks, but feel free to sauté your favorite stir-fry veggies (broccoli, carrots, snap peas) for crunch.

6 ounces thin rice noodles
1 tablespoon toasted sesame oil
1 tablespoon neutral oil (such as vegetable, grapeseed, or sunflower)
1 leek, white and light green parts only, chopped
2 medium cloves garlic, minced
1 tablespoon minced fresh ginger
1 teaspoon red pepper flakes
2 tablespoons red curry paste
2 cups canned unsweetened coconut milk
1 cup vegetable stock

2 teaspoons fish sauce
1 tablespoon honey
Juice of 1 lime
Kosher salt
2 dozen clams, scrubbed
2 dozen mussels, scrubbed and debearded
1 cup packed fresh Thai or regular basil leaves

GARNISH
1 tablespoon chopped fresh chives

Cook the rice noodles according to the package directions. Drain, rinse under cool water, and divide among 4 bowls.

In a large skillet, heat both oils over medium heat. Add the leek, garlic, ginger, pepper flakes, and red curry paste and cook until very fragrant, about 2 minutes. Add the coconut milk, stock, fish sauce, honey, and lime juice and whisk to combine. Season the sauce to taste with salt.

Add the clams and cover. After 5 minutes, add the mussels and basil to the pan and re-cover. Cook until the clams and mussels open up, about 4 to 6 minutes. (Discard any that do not open.) Divide the opened clams and mussels among the bowls of noodles. Evenly pour the red curry sauce over each bowl and garnish with the chopped chives.

Fanfare Tip

Craft a curry of your own by experimenting with other ingredients. Swap in brown rice for the noodles and tender, thinly sliced beef for the seafood. For a vegetarian version, try meaty portobellos and eggplant.

First-Prize Breakfast Sandwich with Orange Lavender Fig Jam

(page 12)

Fig and Brie Frittata with Caramelized Leeks

(page 28)

Grilled Eggplant Banh Mi

(page 50)

Avocado and Heirloom Tomato Gazpacho

(page 64)

Roasted Veggie Crostini with Sunflower Seed–Cream Cheese Pesto

(page 78)

Dilled Meyer Lemon Crab Cake Sliders

(page 84)

**Pulled Buffalo Chicken Tacos
with Red Onions and Poblanos**

(page 122)

Madeira Chicken with Tarragon and Shiitakes

(page 124)

Seared Tuna with Spicy Guava Butter and Crushed Macadamias

(page 132)

Moroccan-Spiced Turkey Meatballs with Coconut Basil Marinara
(page 134)

Lemony Roasted Garlic Kale Caesar with Sesame Croutons

(page 156)

Asian Cabbage Slaw with Watermelon Radishes

(page 170)

White Cheddar and Sage
Buttermilk Biscuits
(page 194)

Kailua Coupe with Balsamic Fig Syrup
(page 198)

Mascarpone and Mint Strawberry Cheesecake Pops

(page 201)

Orange Lavender Fig Jam
(page 217)

Roasted Tomato Aioli
(page 223)

**Sunflower Seed–Cream
Cheese Pesto**
(page 216)

Chapter 5

Going Green

My mom's love for wholesome ingredients inspired my exploration of all things green. She instilled in me a hunger for vegetables of all shapes and sizes, and this chapter is a healthy mix of those nutritious elements.

The Cheese Drawer

Who moved my mom's cheese?

No one, thank goodness. It would certainly put a damper on the evening if we were seconds away from dinner and couldn't find the Drunken Goat. No, this is not what my family calls me. It is, in fact, an essential member of an elite squad of artisanal cheeses that belong to my mom.

Is it just me or did I just invent the intro to Law & Order: Special Cheddars Unit?

My mom is the sage of Saint André, the guru of Gorgonzola, and the prima donna of Parmigiano. I was fortunate to grow up with a mother who has an immaculate palate for epicurean eats. While my dad and I were shaping crab cakes or stuffing lemons into a hen, my mom was at the counter beside us, arranging exquisite greens into a salad bowl like an inspired composer. Her salads were unlike anything my childhood friends had ever seen. They would watch in astonishment as she tossed oddly shaped lettuces—frisée, escarole, endive—with aromatic cheeses, grassy herbs, and vibrant fruits. For me, fresh flecks of floral basil, pungent Caña de Cabra crumbles, and spicy red radicchio were the norm.

But it wasn't just the salads. My mom taught me that this exotic array of cheeses was like a hidden drawer full of tiny delicious friends, eagerly waiting to serve me. On a sleepless morning of fuzzy socks and chamomile tea, my mom would pair juicy ripe strawberries next to thin strips of sharp Vermont cheddar, golden white, calming, and distinctively nutty. If soothing a bad day was needed, she would call on Taleggio from Italy, luxuriously buttery and oozing with fruity funk. And for special occasions, out came the triple crème Explorateur from France, a silky, heavenly gift from a cow who was clearly so full of happiness that he had jumped over the moon to get to my plate.

Some may find serenity in meditation or religion. But as I relive these blissful moments with my magnificent mom, her ambrosial bounty of cheeses, and her beautiful salads, I am suddenly in a state of luscious peace. Where berries and Bucheron live in eternal harmony, and all is right with the world.

★ **Blackberry and Bucheron Salad** (page 154): This salad's spin features my favorite tart fruit paired with mild Bucheron cheese and an orange vinaigrette to wake up the taste buds.

★ **Strawberry and Goat Cheese Crostini with Vanilla-Balsamic Reduction** (page 77): In this whimsical, summer-friendly hors d'oeuvre I've mixed sweet strawberries with fresh, fragrant basil and creamy goat cheese to create a two-bite, salad-like app.

My mom (in 1977, on her honeymoon in France) returns to the scene of the (triple) crème—Paris, the city that originally sparked her lifelong liaison with cheese.

Blackberry and Bucheron Salad

I don't claim to be an epicurean expert, but I do have a flair for *fromage*. Many women spend their spare time in the shoe aisle. As for me—it's the cheese department or bust. I'm a sucker for sophisticated varieties like Bucheron whose flavor profile boasts two personalities in one: a gooey rind, which offers a buttery bite like Brie, and a dense, crumbly middle similar to goat cheese. I sprinkle the tangy white cheese onto my greens along with tart blackberries and toasted pecans.

What do you know—maybe I am a cheese whiz.

½ cup chopped pecans
6 cups baby arugula
1 cup blackberries
3 ounces Bucheron cheese, white center only (see Fanfare Tips), crumbled, or fresh goat cheese

Juice of 1 orange
3 tablespoons good-quality extra-virgin olive oil
Kosher salt and cracked black pepper

In a dry small skillet, toast the pecans over medium-low heat, tossing frequently, until lightly golden and very fragrant, about 5 minutes. Immediately remove the nuts from the pan and transfer to a bowl to stop the cooking process.

In a large bowl, combine the arugula, blackberries, pecans, and half of the crumbled Bucheron. Squeeze the orange and drizzle the olive oil over the salad. Season with a pinch each of salt and pepper and gently toss to combine.

Divide the salad among 4 plates and garnish with the remaining Bucheron and additional cracked pepper.

Fanfare Tips

- The gooey rind of Bucheron doesn't crumble well into salads, but it's great on crackers. Or if you're in a crostini-crafting mood, spread the velvety rind onto toasted baguette slices.
- Bucheron bears a fancy name and look without the fancy price tag, making it a great pick for your next crowd-friendly cheese board. Dress up the platter with a drizzle of honey and fresh herbs.

Cucumber, Mango, and Parsley Salad

Surprise your dinner guests with a salad course that goes above and beyond. Sweet, juicy mango and refreshing cucumber mingle like a charm in this simple yet graceful dish. Frisée is known for being slightly bitter, so I add a nutty, caramel-like maple vinaigrette to round out the flavors.

¼ cup salted roasted pumpkin seeds
1 mango, sliced into ½-inch-thick strips
    (about 1 cup)
1 seedless cucumber, peeled, halved
    lengthwise, and cut on an angle into
    long ½-inch-thick half-moons (about
    1 cup)

2 tablespoons chopped fresh parsley
2 cups frisée lettuce
¼ teaspoon kosher salt
¼ teaspoon coarse black pepper
¾ cup Orange Maple Vinaigrette
    (page 174)

In a dry small skillet, toast the pumpkin seeds over medium-low heat, tossing frequently, until lightly golden and very fragrant, about 5 minutes. Some of the seeds will pop and make a snapping noise. This just means they are toasting correctly. Immediately remove the seeds from the pan and transfer to a bowl to stop the cooking process.

In a large bowl, combine the mango, cucumber, parsley, frisée, salt, and pepper. Several tablespoons at a time, pour the maple vinaigrette over the salad, tossing to combine, until it is dressed to your liking.

Divide the salad among 4 plates and top with the toasted pumpkin seeds.

Fanfare Tip

If frisée is too bold for your palate, go for a mix of mild baby greens instead.

Lemony Roasted Garlic Kale Caesar with Sesame Croutons

Bright acidic lemon, mellow roasted garlic, and tangy Worcestershire fuse to create a dressing that you could eat with a spoon. Kale's sturdy texture is fantastic for sopping up every last drop, and the unexpected crunch and pop of homemade sesame croutons will leave you wondering why you don't eat salads more often.

2 cups torn crusty Italian bread (crouton size)
2 tablespoons olive oil
1 tablespoon unsalted butter, melted
2 teaspoons black sesame seeds
¼ teaspoon kosher salt
¼ teaspoon coarse black pepper
6 cups thinly sliced lacinato kale leaves, ribs removed (about 1 bunch)

Lemony Roasted Garlic Dressing (recipe follows)

GARNISH
¼ cup shaved parmesan cheese
Cracked black pepper

Preheat the oven to 400°F.

Spread the torn bread on a baking sheet. In a small bowl, whisk together the olive oil, melted butter, sesame seeds, salt, and pepper and pour over the bread, tossing with your hands to combine. Bake until the croutons are golden and toasted, 12 to 14 minutes. Reserve the sesame seeds remaining on the bottom of the baking sheet.

In a large bowl, mix the kale and croutons with several tablespoons of the dressing at a time, tossing to combine, until the salad is coated to your liking. Divide the salad among 4 plates and garnish with the shaved parmesan, cracked black pepper, and reserved sesame seeds.

Fanfare Tips

- Caesar doesn't have to stand alone in this palace. Opt for additional yummy toppings like capers, sliced avocados, or marinated artichokes.
- Serve this crisp salad alongside Moroccan-Spiced Turkey Meatballs with Coconut Basil Marinara (page 134) to balance out the rich, warm flavors.

Lemony Roasted Garlic Dressing

MAKES ⅔ CUP

4 small cloves Roasted Garlic (page 225)
1 tablespoon Dijon mustard
2 tablespoons Worcestershire sauce
2 tablespoons grated parmesan cheese

Juice of 1 lemon
Kosher salt and cracked black pepper
⅓ cup olive oil
1 tablespoon plain Greek yogurt

Using the flat side of your knife, mash the roasted garlic until it becomes a paste.

In a deep bowl, combine the roasted garlic paste, mustard, Worcestershire, parmesan, lemon juice, and ¼ teaspoon each salt and pepper. Slowly stream in the olive oil and, using a whisk or a blender, blend well until the dressing is emulsified and thick. Whisk in the yogurt and season to taste with additional salt and pepper.

The Man Behind the Curtain

My parents' house sits just ten minutes from the most magnificent restaurant in Raleigh, North Carolina. When they opened their doors in 1992, Margaux's became our second dining room. The birthdays, the anniversaries, and the Bat Mitzvahs wouldn't have been the same without their phenomenal food and heart-centered individuals who make you feel like part of their family. There is a sense of enchantment about the place, and in their twenty-plus years, they have achieved what most eateries only dream of—the inexplicable ability to grab ahold of you and never let you go.

As a first-time diner, you'd have no trouble identifying their secret: They serve five-star cuisine purified through an unpretentious filter. I'm talking food so good it will either put you in a meditative state or induce a Gene Kelly—esque trance of twirling around light posts and tapping your feet because the grouper was just *that* good. My mom's relationship with their salmon—tender and trickling with frothy, tangy beurre blanc—is like something out of a Nicholas Sparks novel. Except no one dies at the end (well, other than the fish). Their tuna—silken and pink inside and resting on a mountain of velvety polenta—is my dad's one-way ticket to transcendence. And for my sister, it's the rich corn bread infused with honey and slathered with whipped butter.

Here is where the story shifts . . . as to this point I have been addressing Margaux's from a patron's perspective. In college I was asked to choose an internship that corresponded with my major, English. Through the magic of persuasion, and confusing my professor by talking in circles, I was granted consent to pursue my kitchen passion and then write about it. With open arms from owner Steve, I dove headfirst into Margaux's kitchen, where I landed at the feet of an impressive Oz-like statue. Executive chef Andrew—a sturdy, towering figure with

Family friend and Margaux owner, Steve Horowitz (far right), spruces up my Bat Mitzvah buffet at his restaurant in 1998.

wavy blonde hair and a fluffy fistful of cilantro—stared down at me. "Come along then," he declared in a London-flavored accent. "Let's make aioli."

For the next several months, I circulated from station to station and absorbed every ounce of Margaux's artistic creations. I had grown up on their Caesar and was now crafting and hand-tossing this lush, savory dressing with crisp shards of romaine. In the land of appetizers, chef Laura, aficionado of hors d'oeuvres, schooled me on summer rolls. Side by side we would stuff and fold translucent rice paper wrappers with lump crabmeat and tangy pickled vegetables. With each illustrious dish, my inspiration soared. Although Margaux's will always hold a fairy-tale-like fascination for me, this experience exposed the man behind the curtain—as I was now on the other side.

★ **Lemony Roasted Garlic Kale Caesar with Sesame Croutons** (page 156): I have transformed Margaux's creamy, roasty dressing—which fed my life-long Caesar craving—into a citrusy compilation of nutritious kale and nutty croutons.

★ **Ginger and Lemongrass Shrimp Summer Rolls** (page 98): These light, aromatic wraps dipped in velvety coconut peanut sauce honor the legendary fresh rolls I learned in Margaux's kitchen.

Asparagus and Fingerling Salad with Chive Vinaigrette

SERVES 4 AS A SIDE DISH

Don't let the name fool you, we're talking salad with potatoes here, not potato salad. This simple side covers your starch and veggies all in one delicious dish. Vibrant asparagus spears and golden roasted potatoes are dressed in a light chive vinaigrette and topped with shaved radishes for a peppery crunch.

1 pound fingerling potatoes
2 tablespoons olive oil
½ teaspoon kosher salt
½ teaspoon coarse black pepper
1 pound asparagus, ends trimmed
2 tablespoons roughly chopped fresh
　　parsley

Chive Vinaigrette (recipe follows)

GARNISH
¼ cup thinly sliced radishes
¼ cup shaved parmesan cheese
Cracked black pepper

Preheat the oven to 425°F.

Toss the fingerling potatoes with the olive oil, salt, and pepper and spread them onto a baking sheet. Roast the potatoes until they are lightly golden brown and tender, 25 to 30 minutes. Allow the potatoes to cool to room temperature, and then slice them in half.

Bring a large pot of salted water to a boil over high heat. Set up a large bowl filled with ice and water.

Drop the asparagus spears into the boiling water and blanch for 1 minute. Transfer them to the ice water bowl for 30 seconds to stop the cooking, then drain and halve them crosswise.

In a large bowl, toss the potatoes, asparagus, and chopped parsley with the chive vinaigrette. Serve garnished with the radishes, shaved parmesan, and cracked black pepper.

Fanfare Tip

No chives in the herb aisle? Swap in the dark green tops of scallions for the same sharp, oniony bite.

Chive Vinaigrette

MAKES ABOUT ½ CUP

2 tablespoons roughly chopped fresh
    chives
1 tablespoon fresh lemon juice
1 tablespoon Dijon mustard

1 tablespoon champagne vinegar
¼ cup olive oil
Kosher salt and coarse black pepper

In a blender or mini food processor, combine the chives, lemon juice, mustard, and vinegar and pulse to combine. With the motor still running, stream in the olive oil until the vinaigrette is thick and emulsified. Season to taste with salt and pepper.

Chickpea, Fennel, and Mint Salad

Chickpeas deserve more satisfaction than being ground up as the star of hummus. Let them take center stage with their full rounded shape in this citrusy salad featuring fresh, fragrant mint, crunchy fennel, and briny feta. Instead of slicing shallots directly into the mix, these sweet oniony bits are pulsed into a tart vinaigrette.

4½ cups canned chickpeas (three 15-ounce cans), drained and rinsed
1 small fennel bulb, thinly sliced crosswise into strips (about 1 cup)
2 tablespoons chopped fennel fronds

½ cup chopped fresh mint
½ cup crumbled feta cheese
½ cup Grapefruit Shallot Vinaigrette (page 175)

In a large bowl, combine the chickpeas, sliced fennel, fennel fronds, mint, and feta, reserving a few handfuls of mint and feta for the top. Pour several tablespoons of the vinaigrette at a time over the salad, tossing to combine, until it is dressed to your liking.

Refrigerate for 1 hour before serving and garnish with the reserved chopped mint and feta crumbles.

Fanfare Tip

If you're preparing this dish the day before, leave out the mint and fennel fronds and toss those with the dressed salad just before serving. This will keep their refreshing flavor and vibrant green color as bright as possible.

Lime Poppy Seed Slaw

Coleslaw can be a mundane side dish, but I believe it has far more potential. A zippy boost of lime zest gives this crunchy cabbage an unexpected burst of citrus, while poppy seeds offer a sweet, nutty snap. Slaw is sensational solo—say that five times fast—but I prefer it stuffed inside good-quality rye bread. Top it with sliced turkey, Swiss cheese, and FAN Sauce (page 137) and you've just created a yummy homemade Rachel.

Or *Rachael*, depending on who your hero is.

8 to 10 cups shredded green cabbage
(about one 3-pound cabbage)
2 cups shredded carrots
1 cup plain Greek yogurt
½ cup mayonnaise
3 tablespoons apple cider vinegar

1 tablespoon honey
Grated zest and juice of 1 lime
½ teaspoon kosher salt
¼ teaspoon coarse black pepper
2 teaspoons poppy seeds

In a very large bowl, combine the cabbage and carrots. In a separate bowl, whisk together the yogurt, mayonnaise, vinegar, honey, lime zest, lime juice, salt, pepper, and 1 teaspoon of the poppy seeds. Add half of the dressing to the cabbage mixture and toss. Continue adding the dressing, tossing as you pour, until the slaw is coated to your liking.

Transfer the dressed slaw to a clean bowl, cover, and refrigerate for at least 2 hours and preferably overnight.

Just before serving, top the slaw with the remaining 1 teaspoon poppy seeds.

Fanfare Tip

To shred or not to shred? Store-bought shredded cabbage is a great quick fix for slaw. However, if you're making this dish in bulk and need plenty of cabbage to go around, you might find that the "convenient" solution isn't exactly wallet-friendly. The answer: Sift through your storage to find those food processor attachments you didn't know what to do with. Pop on the shredding or slicing disc for piles of fresh cabbage in no time.

The Friday Special

Pull up a chair, or possibly a sandwich, for we are about to embark on an epic tale of lunch. A bread-time story, if you will, of pickles and coleslaw and rye—oh my!

Grandparents have many different methods of demonstrating their love. One of the various ways mine would express their adoration was through sandwiches. Creamy, tangy coleslaw dripping from rye bread transports me back to their New Jersey home, where my grandfather, "Poppy," first taught me how to use mustard. Although we moved to North Carolina when I was four, we frequently flew north for a visit to Springfield. Our arrival was always trademarked by two things: my grandmother "Bea Bea" in the kitchen window bunched together with my great-aunt Annette, both eagerly clapping banana-colored dish gloves, and a tremendous takeout lunch from the Millburn Deli.

Inside this nearby sandwich staple emporium was a world ruled by juicy Russian dressing, Friday Specials, and Turkey Joes. I can still smell the thick, briny,

A recent photo of Bea Bea and me enjoying a winter lunch at the Millburn Deli.

ridge-cut pickles carefully placed atop each Friday Special triple-decker—over-stuffed with creamy tuna and egg salad and cut into thirds. I can still taste the Turkey Joe's thin, delicate ovals of rye bread—lightly buttered and loaded with nutty Swiss and decadent slaw.

I can say with absolute certainty that my grandmother will celebrate the official release of this cookbook by announcing it to each and every patron at the Millburn Deli that day. For decades we have gathered around these soulful sandwiches, once even via FedEx for my twenty-first birthday. (*Yes, my grandmother mailed me a sandwich.*) These wax paper–wrapped memories feel as near to me as my adoring grandparents—who cherished each of us in our own unique way. So today as I craft various concoctions of cabbage or plunk cucumbers into a vinegary brine, my kitchen disappears and I resurface in Springfield, New Jersey.

---

* **Lime Poppy Seed Slaw** (page 163): I punch up the citrus and add a pop of crunchy black specks in this sassy slaw.

* **Asian Cabbage Slaw with Watermelon Radishes** (page 170): I toss colorful, spicy radishes with salty soy and sharp ginger for this tasty mix.

* **Garlicky Dill Pickles** (page 196): I infuse oniony flavor and the herby floral sweetness of dill to create these crisp, addictive bites.

Rustic Panzanella with Olive Vinaigrette

I once tried to eat my copy of *Under the Tuscan Sun*. It didn't work. In my next attempt to satisfy my Italian craving, I prepared this dish. Panzanella is a chunky vegetable salad typically made with stale bread soaked in a yummy vinegar-based dressing. My version of this refreshing Tuscan treat calls for homemade garlicky croutons, salty feta, and a bright briny olive vinaigrette.

¼ to ⅓ cup olive oil

2 medium cloves garlic, gently smashed but still intact

4 cups cubed (1-inch) country-style bread, such as ciabatta or pain de campagne ★

½ teaspoon kosher salt

¼ teaspoon coarse black pepper

2 pounds vine-ripened or Roma (plum) tomatoes, seeded and cut into 1-inch chunks

1 yellow bell pepper, cut into 1-inch chunks

1 green bell pepper, cut into 1-inch chunks

1 large seedless cucumber, peeled and cut into 1-inch chunks

6 ounces crumbled feta cheese

½ cup packed fresh basil leaves

Olive Vinaigrette (recipe follows)

In a large skillet, heat ¼ cup of the olive oil and the garlic cloves over medium heat until the cloves are a light golden brown color, 3 to 5 minutes. Remove with a slotted spoon and discard.

Add the bread cubes to the garlic oil and season them with the salt and black pepper. Sauté the bread, adding more oil if needed and tossing frequently, until golden brown on all sides, 8 to 10 minutes. Let the croutons cool to room temperature.

★ The first time I wandered into an international specialty foods shop, I was mesmerized by the radiant dishes that lined the display cases. One in particular caught my eye: a hearty, Tuscan-inspired, multicolored mixture of peppers, tomatoes, and cucumbers. I treated myself to a sample and then went home to create my very own adaptation—with the addition of torn pita bread for texture. My head spun with excitement as I believed I had just conceived a colossal one-of-a-kind recipe. As it turns out, panzanella dates back to the sixteenth century. Being naïve is fun.

In a large bowl, combine the croutons, tomatoes, bell peppers, cucumber, and feta. Gently tear in the basil leaves. Pour the olive vinaigrette, a few tablespoons at a time, over the veggies and gently toss until the salad is dressed to your liking. Refrigerate for 30 minutes to 1 hour before serving.

Olive Vinaigrette

MAKES ¾ CUP

¼ cup champagne vinegar
⅓ cup pitted Manzanilla olives
1 tablespoon fresh lemon juice
2 teaspoons Dijon mustard

2 teaspoons honey
⅓ to ½ cup olive oil
Kosher salt and coarse black pepper

In a mini food processor or blender, pulse the vinegar, olives, lemon juice, mustard, and honey until smooth. With the motor still running, slowly stream in ⅓ cup of the olive oil. If the vinaigrette is still slightly chunky and has not fully come together, add the remaining oil, a few drops at a time, until the vinaigrette is thoroughly emulsified. Season to taste with salt and pepper.

Fanfare Tip

Salad is difficult to eat in the car, so here's how you take this panzanella for the ride. Stuff the chunky, marinated mixture into a whole wheat pita for easy on-the-go eating. It may seem odd to stuff bread salad into bread, but as the wise Soulja Boy once said, "Snacks on snacks on snacks." Spread on some hummus for added protein.

The Chopsticks Waltz

Up until 1995, the tooth fairy had apparently lost my address.

When I was four years old, all my friends began to lose their teeth. One wrong wiggle on the playground and out another would fall. They would prance around making their dental declaration to the world while I sat quietly nearby, fully-toothed and feeling left out.

I was ten years old when my first tooth came flying out with a bite of lamb chop. Most kids got a quarter in exchange for their original tooth. I got twenty dollars and a party at the local Japanese steak house. Despite the missing piece from my mouth, I ordered all of my favorites—the crisp, zesty salad, the enormous buttery shrimp, and the generous pile of soy-glazed zucchini. Each dish clearly required a sturdy set of chompers, but I could have been toothless and still made my way to the tempura ice cream at the finish line.

Every town has its own teppanyaki-style restaurant, and Raleigh's local hibachi-lovers' dream was Kanki. I have spent countless hours feasting inside their teriyaki-scented walls, as I lived in Raleigh for the majority of my life. Kanki was the place to be for birthdays, first dates, graduations, and naturally, celebrations of lost teeth. Each table stretched to seat nearly a dozen people, and it was common to mingle with strangers. I remember as kids we were given chopsticks secured with rubber bands (and how conveniently those training-wheeled utensils fit inside our nostrils). By high school, we were distracted by our colossal Nokia cell phones and had graduated from sodas to virgin daiquiris. In college, we would label our white to-go boxes so that the leftovers wouldn't get mixed up in the fridge when we would desperately return for them at 2:00 a.m. after a long night of "studying."

Although Kanki has served me infinite years of memories, I must confess—it's the food that's fed my soul.

I may have participated in—and technically led—the chopsticks-up-the-nose skit, but the moment the salad arrived I was all business. Even at ten, I recall savor-

As it turns out, chopsticks are for more than just sticking up your nose. Here, I present a drumroll on the flattop grill at Kanki to a tableful of mostly strangers. Moments later, I would be shooed away by the waitress. (I'm considering sending her a signed copy of this book.)

ing each spicy bite of ginger dressing that coated the layers of cold, crunchy iceberg. Around the table at seventeen, I played "too cool" for everything but was secretly taking flavor notes so I wouldn't forget the luscious clarified butter I saw splashed onto the steaming flattop with briny shrimp and perfectly marbled steak. In college, I sipped light Japanese beers and chatted philosophy, but I stared past the oversize steel can to study the chef searing yakisoba noodles in a smoky vapor of garlic and sesame oil.

So to my friends who have dined with me on a regular basis over the years and wondered why I could never wipe the dazed expression from my face, *now you know why.*

Or at least, let's just pretend that's why.

★ **Creamy Ginger Dressing** (page 171): This chunky dressing from my childhood was bright and vibrant. I have reimagined it as more of a creamy vinaigrette—flowing with assertive horseradish and loads of lemon.

★ **Spicy Soba Noodles with Shrimp and Hoisin** (page 146): After noodling around for the perfect flavors, I have spotlighted my stir-fry with thick, barbecue-like hoisin and a daring dash of tangy fish sauce.

Asian Cabbage Slaw with Watermelon Radishes

Life is beautiful. Did I say life? I meant watermelon radishes. These slightly sweet, emerald and pink–hued splendors add a fresh, peppery bite to this Asian-inspired slaw. Speckled with homemade peanuts and doused in a tangy blend of toasted sesame oil and fragrant ginger, this crunchy cabbage is an umami explosion.

1 small head green cabbage, thinly sliced (about 4 cups)

4 medium watermelon radishes, sliced into matchsticks (about 1 cup)

1 tablespoon black and white sesame seeds

Honey-Roasted Rosemary and Black Pepper Peanuts (page 108), roughly chopped

2 tablespoons rice vinegar

1 tablespoon lower-sodium soy sauce

1 tablespoon toasted sesame oil

1 tablespoon honey

1 teaspoon minced fresh ginger

¼ cup neutral oil (such as vegetable, grapeseed, or sunflower)

In a large bowl, combine the cabbage, radishes, sesame seeds, and chopped peanuts.

In a small bowl, whisk together the rice vinegar, soy sauce, toasted sesame oil, honey, and ginger. Whisking vigorously, stream in the neutral oil until the vinaigrette is thoroughly emulsified.

Several tablespoons at a time, pour the vinaigrette over the slaw until it is saturated to your liking. Toss well to combine the flavors. Refrigerate for at least 1 hour before serving.

Flippidy-Doo's

- For a sweet and spicy Asian spin on the classic fish taco, marinate sushi-grade tuna with minced ginger and soy sauce and give it a quick sear. Top warmed flour tortillas with the still-pink slices and bring the heat with Sriracha and the sweet with this slaw.
- Speaking of fish tacos, the bright fragrant flavors of this slaw make it an excellent topper for Fish Tacos with Pickled Radishes and Grilled Pineapple Aioli (page 142).

Creamy Ginger Dressing

I can never decide what's more fun at a Japanese steak house, the crunchy greens covered in tangy dressing or watching the tableside chefs fling shrimp into their hats. Instead of dining out for your next Asian craving, grab your chopsticks and head for home because we're crafting a zesty ginger vinaigrette—bursting with light, acidic rice vinegar and a kick of heat from horseradish—right in your very own kitchen.

And like my friend Fergie says: "A little sake never hurt nobody."

1½ tablespoons minced fresh ginger
1 medium clove garlic, minced
1 teaspoon horseradish
1 tablespoon Dijon mustard
2 tablespoons fresh lemon juice
3 tablespoons rice vinegar

1½ teaspoons honey
2 teaspoons lower-sodium soy sauce
1 tablespoon plain Greek yogurt
¼ cup neutral oil (such as vegetable, grapeseed, or sunflower)
Kosher salt and coarse black pepper

In a blender or food processor, pulse the ginger, garlic, horseradish, mustard, lemon juice, vinegar, honey, soy sauce, and Greek yogurt until thoroughly combined. With the motor still running, stream in the oil until the dressing is thick and emulsified. Season to taste with salt and pepper.

Flippidy-Doo's

- For an Asian spin on chicken salad, whisk a few extra tablespoons of Greek yogurt into this dressing to soften up the flavors. Toss with shredded chicken and crunchy scallions and serve alongside romaine leaves for a tasty take on lettuce wraps. So flavorful—no dipping sauce required.
- For an easy bowl of Asian-inspired greens to partner with Rice Noodles with Citrus Peanut Sauce (page 114), toss this dressing with shredded napa cabbage, carrot ribbons, and toasted almonds.

Grapefruit Vinaigrette with Orange Blossom Honey and Basil

MAKES 1½ CUPS

In this sweet, floral vinaigrette, tart grapefruit juice blends with fresh basil and orange blossom–infused honey. Did you know you could accomplish elegance with just five ingredients? Now you do. Share the love, my friend.

And by love, I mean salad.

Juice of 1 grapefruit ★ (about ¾ cup)
3 tablespoons chopped fresh basil
1 tablespoon orange blossom honey

1 tablespoon white balsamic vinegar
Kosher salt and coarse black pepper
¼ cup olive oil

In a small bowl, whisk together the grapefruit juice, basil, honey, vinegar, ¼ teaspoon salt, and ⅛ teaspoon pepper. Slowly whisk in the oil until the vinaigrette is emulsified and thoroughly combined. Adjust the seasoning with salt and pepper.

Fanfare Tip

Experiment with different honeys. Sample sweet unique flavors like wildflower, sourwood, and any regional variety you can get your hands on. It's always best to support local. It's good for your soul (and your allergies).

Most kids prefer orange juice, but I couldn't get enough of the sharp juicy tang of grapefruit. I remember the special ridged spoon my mom would hand me to pluck out each triangular nook. I remember how every acidic bite made my mouth water. I still adore grapefruit today, and I've found that the flavor adds an unexpected tartness to simple vinaigrettes. I *squeeze* it in as often as possible. Yes, I know. I'm very punny.

Herby Buttermilk Dill Dressing

I'm going to tell you a little secret—about yourself. You love ranch. It's okay, so do I. It may not be the lightest option on the table or the lowest in fat but *dammit, it is delicious*. Of course we all reach for the raspberry balsamic in public when we're pretending to be adults, but you and I both know the truth. I vote we raise our salad forks in protest and say, "No more!" No more will we feel shame in enjoying ranch dressing's creamy goodness. Why? Because *this* ranch is different. With fresh herbs, tart citrus, and the light addition of Greek yogurt, this is a ranch to be proud of. ★

½ cup plain Greek yogurt
¼ cup mayonnaise or sour cream
¼ cup buttermilk
2 tablespoons finely chopped fresh chives
    or the dark green tops of scallions
2 teaspoons finely chopped fresh dill
2 teaspoons finely chopped fresh parsley
2 teaspoons fresh lemon juice
1 medium clove garlic, grated
1 teaspoon Worcestershire sauce
Kosher salt and coarse black pepper

In a small bowl, whisk together the yogurt, mayonnaise, buttermilk, chives, dill, parsley, lemon juice, garlic, Worcestershire, and ¼ teaspoon each salt and pepper. Adjust the seasoning with salt and pepper.

Flippidy-Doo

Double the batch and transform your remaining ranch into three new dressings:
- Whisk in sweet, nutty Roasted Garlic (page 225) for a creamy sauce to drizzle over burgers.
- Stir in your favorite hot sauce to make a spicy dip for fries.
- Blend in avocado for a silky dressing to ladle over greens.

★ Typical schoolchildren carry around a book bag. I walked the preschool halls with a bear named Sasha in one hand and a security blanket of ranch dressing in the other. School was lost on me, but from my earliest snack-time memories—crunchy celery spears dunked into the creamy, herbaceous dressing—I was comforted by the lingering flavors of chives, buttermilk, and black pepper. As I grew up and out of my tomboy style, it was the only accessory that followed me through my teenage years and beyond. From a partner in crime for chicken fingers to a garlicky landing zone for dunking my sandwiches, ranch played the Hobbes to my Calvin. In my lightened-up version of the savory, addictive dressing I opt for an abundant amount of fresh herbs and tart Greek yogurt.

Orange Maple Vinaigrette

Stop buying salad dressing. Seriously, stop it. Whisk this one up in your own kitchen, and I promise you'll put down the bottle for good. Rich maple syrup makes all the difference in this made-from-scratch dressing. Bright orange balances out the acidity of tangy white balsamic vinegar, while sweet, woody maple syrup rounds out both flavors to make this a four-ingredient vinaigrette to remember.

Juice of 2 oranges
2 tablespoons white balsamic vinegar
2 tablespoons pure maple syrup or maple agave

Kosher salt and cracked black pepper
½ cup olive oil

In a large bowl or a jar with a tight lid,★ combine the orange juice, vinegar, maple syrup, ¼ teaspoon salt, and ⅛ teaspoon pepper. If you're using a bowl, slowly stream in the oil, whisking vigorously to combine. If you're using a jar, add the oil and shake the ingredients together until the oil is emulsified. Adjust the seasoning with salt and pepper.

Fanfare Tips

- When making a vinaigrette, a 3-to-1 ratio for olive oil to vinegar is standard—unless you favor vinegar's bright acidic punch like me. If you do, but fear going overboard—try out your heavy-handedness with lighter, less intense varieties of vinegar like white balsamic, champagne, or sherry vinegar.
- Real maple syrup can be costly, so keep an eye out for maple agave. It packs the same amber punch without the price tag.

★ Dijon mustard jars will always hold a special place in my heart. My mom would cleverly repurpose the empty glass jars as vehicles for the homemade vinaigrettes that dressed our salads each night at dinner. A few splashes of olive oil, a dash of vinegar, a squeeze of lemon—it was *shake and make*. And I helped.

Grapefruit Shallot Vinaigrette

Who elected lemon the president of vinaigrette? Don't be shy with your salad's citrus: Explore other bright flavors like grapefruit to produce a tart, tangy dressing to pair with mixed greens. For a mild oniony flavor without the sharp bite, this vinaigrette calls for shallots blended right into the mix.

¼ cup champagne vinegar or white wine vinegar
½ cup fresh grapefruit juice (about 1 large grapefruit)
1 tablespoon Dijon mustard

1 small shallot, minced (about 2 tablespoons)
2 tablespoons honey
Kosher salt and coarse black pepper
¼ cup olive oil

In a blender or mini food processor, pulse together the vinegar, grapefruit juice, mustard, shallot, honey, and ¼ teaspoon each salt and pepper. With the motor still running, stream in the oil until the vinaigrette is fully emulsified. Adjust the seasoning with salt and pepper.

Fanfare Tip

Invest that dollar you found in your back pocket by purchasing a plastic squeeze bottle to keep tasty vinaigrettes like this one on hand in the fridge for quick salads during the week.

Chapter 6

Sideways

*There are no cameos on my plate, as every element has its own starring role.
From garlic-scented roasted asparagus to horseradish-infused root veggies,
these sideways sides are an entrée's best friend.*

Vice Mashed Potato President

You know when you become a grown-up and that spoonful of mashed potatoes no longer arrives at the foot of your bed?

No? Let me elaborate.

Growing up, on many nights, the earthy aroma of boiling potatoes and the nutty smell of slow-roasted garlic would travel upstairs. And so would my dad. Three spoons in hand, he would voyage from room to room offering my mom, sister, and me stolen samples of the meal that was to come. This was a nightly routine that has left me with countless delicious memories containing no more than a mouthful. I remember the juicy single forkfuls of herby roast chicken. I remember the sweet solitary scraps of crab that had fallen astray from their cakes. But most of all, I remember the mashed potatoes.

One fluffy spoonful of the silken, butter-whipped mash and the tensions of the day would fade. Not that I carried much stress as a twelve-year-old other

Here I am, the vice mashed potato president, at age eight (and in my favorite dish gloves), using a meat tenderizer to stomp spuds.

than accidentally sitting on my glasses, but this predinner promo was a wonderful hint of what the near future would hold. It was like the twenty minutes of movie previews before the show. Whether my mom was organizing her Tibetan rock collection, my sister was scribbling in her diary, or I was making a paper birthday crown for the cat . . . the moment we heard my dad's footsteps, we deflected from our activities to savor that one bite.

At a younger age, my culinary curiosity was often sidetracked by alternate hobbies like cutting my own bangs or "doing my homework." But as I grew up I began to spend more time in the kitchen. Before I knew it, my dad offered me the prestigious role of Vice Mashed Potato President. He trusted me with a splash of milk here or a dab of butter there. By smashing and seasoning the spuds and playing a key role in our dinner, I felt a sense of importance in the kitchen early on in life. It led me to have faith in my palate and ultimately create my very own unique fluffy concoctions for all the world to sample.

★ **Rosemary Parsnip Puree with Goat Cheese and Roasted Garlic** (page 180): I've transformed traditional rich, luscious mashed potatoes into a light-as-air parsnip puree laced with nutty roasted garlic and the woody essence of rosemary.

Rosemary Parsnip Puree with Goat Cheese and Roasted Garlic

What the heck is a parsnip? I'm glad you asked. From its outside appearance, it is the carrot's albino cousin. Packed with more nutrients and slightly less carbs than a potato, these root veggies make a delicious creamy side that no one will know isn't their beloved mashed potatoes. I blend them with smooth goat cheese and sweet, mellow roasted garlic to make this light, velvety puree.

1 pound parsnips, peeled and cut into 2-inch chunks
4 sprigs fresh rosemary
3 cloves Roasted Garlic (page 225)
2 tablespoons unsalted butter

2 ounces goat cheese
1 tablespoon half-and-half
1 teaspoon honey
Kosher salt and coarse black pepper
1 tablespoon olive oil

In a large pot, combine the parsnips and rosemary with cold salted water to cover. Bring to a boil over high heat, then reduce the heat to medium-high and simmer the parsnips until very tender, 18 to 20 minutes. Reserve ⅓ cup of the starchy cooking water, drain the parsnips, and throw away the rosemary stems.

Using the flat side of your knife, mash the roasted garlic until it becomes a paste.

In a food processor, combine the roasted garlic paste, parsnips, butter, goat cheese, half-and-half, honey, and ¼ teaspoon each salt and pepper. Add a few tablespoons at a time of the reserved cooking water until the puree is smooth. With the motor still running, stream in the olive oil until the mixture is velvety and whipped. Season to taste with salt and pepper.

Fanfare Tip

Swap other flavors into this puree so that it pleases your specific palate. Earthy herbs like thyme and sage make great green additions, and for a funky kick, swap out the goat cheese for tangy Gorgonzola.

Horseradish and Sage Root Vegetable Mash

Root veggies are a phenomenal way to sneak some nourishment onto your non-vegetable-eater's plate. When mashed, they take on a creamy consistency similar to that of potatoes. In this buttery tangle of vegetables, the zip of fresh, spicy horseradish and warm, woody sage add an unexpected background flavor. Impress your family and friends by teaching them that horseradish comes from a stalky root—not a jar.

½ pound parsnips, peeled and cut into 1-inch cubes
½ pound rutabaga, peeled and cut into 1-inch cubes
½ pound turnips, peeled and cut into 1-inch cubes
½ pound Yukon Gold potatoes, peeled and cut into 1-inch cubes

1 tablespoon chopped fresh sage
1 tablespoon grated fresh horseradish
4 tablespoons (½ stick) unsalted butter
¼ cup half-and-half
Kosher salt and coarse black pepper
1 tablespoon olive oil

In a large pot, combine the parsnips, rutabaga, turnips, and potatoes with cold salted water to cover. Bring to a boil and cook until the vegetables are very soft and tender, 20 to 25 minutes. Drain and then return the vegetables to the pot off the heat.

Add the sage, ½ tablespoon of the horseradish, the butter, half-and-half, and ½ teaspoon each salt and pepper and mash the veggies with a potato masher until smooth. *Note: Horseradish's flavor amplifies as it sits, so if the spicy kick seems subtle—give it a few minutes before grating in another ½ tablespoon.* Adjust the seasoning with salt and pepper.

Scoop into a large bowl, drizzle with the oil, and serve.

Fanfare Tip

Digging the horseradish but not the root veg? Swap out the parsnips, rutabaga, and turnips for all Yukon Golds to create a spicy, creamy spin on traditional mashed taters.

Asparagus School

We frequently had Gus for dinner.

I'm not referring to a family friend, neighbor, or coworker—"Gus" was our nickname for the crunchy green spears that would decorate our dinner plates. They say your Bat Mitzvah is when you become an adult, but I believe I advanced past adolescence the evening my dad taught me proper asparagus etiquette. While tilting my head at a precise angle and dangling Gus just above eye level, there at our very kitchen table, I received my degree in Culinary Consumption. After gently lowering the stem from sky to mouth, several buttery chomps later I had passed with flying green colors. My parents and sister beamed with glee. This was the type of school they were very serious about.

But it wasn't just a crash course in playfulness; this was also an academy of artisanal flavors. Asparagus joined us for dinner alongside family favorites like citrus seared scallops and grilled eggplant lasagna. It wouldn't have been the

Pop quiz day at Asparagus School. #nailedit

same without them. I remember every delicate snap and burst of freshness, and how it was Gus who allowed us to shamelessly master the art of being silly at the dinner table.

★ **Asparagus with Roasted Garlic Butter** (page 184): After a quick dip in the blanching pot, my dad would sauté asparagus in a light bath of butter and sharp minced garlic. In this recipe, I hang on to those key ingredients but opt for basting and roasting instead. I smear smoky asparagus with nutty roasted garlic butter and finish with bright lemon zest to perk up the warm flavors.

★ **Asparagus and Fingerling Salad with Chive Vinaigrette** (page 160): For another play on the pairing of asparagus and garlic, I toss creamy finger-lings and the stalky veg with an herby, oniony chive vinaigrette.

★ **Creamy Roasted Asparagus and Mint Soup** (page 65): My dad would often finish asparagus with fragrant herbs to add a floral note to their meaty flavor. I've gone one step further and blended them with bright mint for a light, velvety soup.

Asparagus with Roasted Garlic Butter

Asparagus is an ideal sidekick for any meal. It's effortless to prepare in bulk, roasts quickly, and easily takes on flavor. In this dish, the spears are slathered with sweet, nutty roasted garlic butter and topped with bright lemon zest.

½ head Roasted Garlic (page 225)
4 tablespoons (½ stick) unsalted butter, melted
2 pounds asparagus, ends trimmed

½ teaspoon kosher salt
¼ teaspoon coarse black pepper
1 teaspoon grated lemon zest

Preheat the oven to 425°F.

Using the flat side of your knife, mash the roasted garlic into a paste. Whisk the garlic paste into the melted butter.

Spread the asparagus on a baking sheet in one even layer. Brush half of the roasted garlic butter onto the spears and season them with the salt and pepper. Roast the asparagus until crisp-tender, 15 to 18 minutes.

While they're still hot, brush the asparagus with the remaining roasted garlic butter and top with the lemon zest.

Flippidy-Doo

Transform these garlicky stalks into a gorgeous garnish by stacking them over Turkey Hash with Baked Runny Eggs (page 30). Poke the yolks just before serving.

Fanfare Tip

Spice it up. Whisk 1 teaspoon of red pepper flakes into your roasted garlic butter for a fantastic fiery flavor.

Somewhere Over the Rainbow Chard Sauté

Sautéed greens are a vibrant, nourishing complement to any meal. This isn't the time when I tell you we eat with our eyes first (although that *is* true), but it is the part where I share my beliefs about eating the rainbow. Chard, that is. I pack my daily plate full of color—not just because it's pretty to look at, but because I want in on all of nature's nutrient-rich ingredients. In this multicolored spectacle of a side, sweet, delicate leeks are sautéed with crunchy chard stems and leaves. Perfect for any dinnertime protein and exceptionally exceptional alongside buttery fried eggs.

1 tablespoon olive oil
½ tablespoon unsalted butter
1 medium clove garlic, minced
1 large bunch rainbow chard, stems and leaves separated and roughly chopped

1 cup chopped leeks, white and light green parts only (about 2 leeks)
1 teaspoon honey
Kosher salt and coarse black pepper

In a large skillet, heat the olive oil and butter over medium heat. Add the garlic, chard stems, leeks, and honey and season generously with salt and pepper. Sauté until the leeks are translucent and the chard stems are tender, 5 to 8 minutes. Add the chard leaves and cook until they wilt, about 1 minute.

Flippidy-Doo

For a plate that pops with cheerful colors, use these greens as a base for Seared Tuna with Spicy Guava Butter and Crushed Macadamias (page 132).

Fanfare Tip

Chard stems can be somewhat bitter, so they need to be thoroughly cooked. Snag one from the pan before serving. If it's still got a pungent bite, swirl some additional honey into the mix.

A Kale of Two Cities

My mom has been a kale connoisseur since before kale was the new . . . kale. Most kids are familiar with the expression "mom jeans." In my family, the term was "mom greens." Not only did my mom's closet boast hip-hugging apparel far from the typical high-waisted denim, but she had mastered the art of nature's green superfoods in every size, shape, and hue. In another life her Indian name was probably Dances with Lettuce or Chants with Chard. Without her guidance, a healthy respect for fresh, natural foods might have flown right over my head.

While many moms I knew spent their days at a local country club, my mom often reveled in foraging for greens up and down the aisles at Whole Foods. As I would assist in unloading the glossy produce bags, I couldn't help but wonder why we needed so many different types of lettuce. Out of curiosity, I once offered my inquiry and received a lengthy tutorial on the difference between escarole and arugula. Although I zoned out somewhere around spinach, it delighted me to see the bliss on my mom's face as she shared her passion for nutritious eating with me. I became more intrigued and quietly began to study her every leafy move.

Many mornings my mom would stand over a sizzling skillet in her nightgown. While most moms were crisping bacon, mine was sautéing golden, browned leeks with red, green, or rainbow chard to partner with her dreamily drippy over-easy eggs. With one hand on a spatula and the other waving an enormous ribbed leaf through the air, she would excitedly shout "Chard!" in my direction, as if she had just unearthed the misplaced key to the universe. I would skip around her in my fuzzy socks and oversize pajamas proudly flapping my own flag—sliced bologna—and egging on her boisterous mantra. "Chard!" we would howl together, as if we were two gowned mental patients who had escaped to a nearby kitchen.

My present-day love for powerhouse greens is truly credited to my mom, who would eat a small forest if it could fit on her plate. She taught me how these

Before my curiosity for greens and veggies was sparked, I followed a strict diet of peanut butter toast and was very fond of breakfast in bed.

Mom leading her own version of the symphony. Here, she conducts a rainbow of vegetables with a spatula to the tune of Tchaikovsky's "Waltz of the Flowers."

nourishing foods could even serve as the epicenter of a meal when blended with other interesting ingredients. Through her artistic eyes, she showed me how to harmonize food textures and colors on a plate's blank canvas. This creative culinary vision was one of her many rare gifts I was fortunate to acquire, and that's one "mom gene" I'm cool with inheriting.

- ★ **Somewhere Over the Rainbow Chard Sauté** (page 185): A sharp tang from garlic gives these vivid greens a zesty spirit.

- ★ **Kale and Parmesan Soup** (page 66): Nutrient-rich kale wilts down to finish this light, brothy soup that's packed with healthy goodness.

Smoky Potato Salad with Charred Scallion Vinaigrette

SERVES 4

In this smoky summertime side, diced spuds take a dive into salty bacon fat and then go for a ride in the oven. (Hey, if you could swim in bacon, you would, too.) Tossed with sweet shallot, crunchy celery, and a light roasted scallion vinaigrette, this mayo-free potato salad brings something fresh to the picnic table.

1 small bunch scallions, trimmed but whole
½ cup olive oil
Kosher salt and coarse black pepper
1¼ pounds red potatoes
3 slices bacon
2 stalks celery with leafy tops, diced

1 small shallot, diced
2 tablespoons chopped fresh dill
¼ cup champagne vinegar
2 tablespoons fresh lemon juice
1 teaspoon honey
1 teaspoon Dijon mustard

Preheat the oven to 400°F.

On a baking sheet, drizzle the scallions with 1 tablespoon of the olive oil and season with salt and pepper. Roast until golden and lightly charred, 15 to 20 minutes. Leave the oven on.

Meanwhile, in a large pot, combine the potatoes with cold salted water to cover. Bring to a boil over high heat, then reduce to a simmer and cook until tender but not fully cooked, 6 to 8 minutes. Drain the potatoes, cool for several minutes, and then roughly chop into ½-inch chunks.

Fanfare Tip

If you're making this side for a big group, cut your time in half by avoiding some of the chopping. Look for peewee potatoes. These tiny, bite-size nuggets boil up quickly (2 to 4 minutes) and are so small you can eat them whole.

In a large skillet, cook the bacon over medium heat until crisp. Drain the slices on paper towels, then roughly chop. Add the diced potatoes to the bacon fat, season with salt and pepper, and toss several times to coat.

Spread the potatoes evenly on a baking sheet and roast, tossing once halfway through, until the potatoes are golden brown and fully cooked, 15 to 18 minutes.

In a large bowl, combine the roasted potatoes, bacon, celery, shallot, and dill.

In a blender or food processor, pulse the roasted scallions, vinegar, lemon juice, honey, and mustard until smooth. With the motor still running, stream in the remaining 7 tablespoons of olive oil, a few tablespoons at a time, until the vinaigrette is thoroughly emulsified. Season to taste with salt and pepper.

Pour the vinaigrette over the potato salad several tablespoons at a time, tossing to combine until it is dressed to your liking. Serve warm or chilled.

Agave-Glazed Baby Carrots with Caraway

That distinctive flavor in rye bread you can't put your finger on? That's caraway. This aromatic, crunchy seed adds an unexpected pop of flavor to these sweet oven-roasted carrots. Serve this sensational side with any weeknight protein, or multiply the amount for a feast fit for a holiday.

1 pound baby carrots, green stems trimmed short
1 tablespoon unsalted butter, melted
2 tablespoons agave
½ teaspoon kosher salt
¼ teaspoon coarse black pepper

½ teaspoon ground caraway seeds ★ (or roughly chop the whole seeds with a knife)
1 tablespoon chopped fresh dill
1 teaspoon grated orange zest

Preheat the oven to 425°F.

Arrange the carrots in an even layer on a baking sheet. In a small bowl, whisk the melted butter with the agave and then pour the mixture over the carrots. Season them with the salt, pepper, and caraway seeds and toss to thoroughly coat.

Roast the carrots until they are lightly browned and caramelized, tossing once halfway through, 20 to 25 minutes. While the carrots are still warm, toss them with the fresh dill and orange zest.

Fanfare Tip

Keep an eye out in the springtime for heirloom carrots. These rainbow-tinted beauties add vibrancy to the simplest of dishes. Try glazing them with local honey instead of agave or garnishing with basil instead of dill.

★ One whiff of caraway's prickly anise scent and I'm tugged through time on a magic rye-bread ride. There are slaw-packed, sloppy Turkey Joe sandwiches from the Millburn Deli in New Jersey with my grandparents. There are cloth-lined baskets brimming with thin golden slices of the nutty toasted bread, which my dad insisted we use to swipe our stuffed cabbage plates clean. To revive these munchable memories and let myself once again get carried away by caraway, I sprinkle the earthy seed throughout my life, my kitchen, and my carrots.

Sweet Potato Fries with Ginger and Spiced Brown Sugar

Not to hate on sliced bread, but I think they should change the expression to "the greatest invention since sweet potato fries." In this un-fried fry recipe, the baked orange wedges are covered in peppery ginger and a sweet and savory spice blend. The recipe feeds 4 to 6, but you'll want to count yourself twice.

2 tablespoons light brown sugar
2 teaspoons chili powder
2 teaspoons kosher salt
1 teaspoon cayenne pepper
1 teaspoon coarse black pepper
1 teaspoon garlic powder

4 medium sweet potatoes (about 8 ounces each), cut lengthwise into ½-inch-thick wedges
¼ cup olive oil
1 tablespoon minced fresh ginger

Preheat the oven to 425°F. Grease a baking sheet.

In a small bowl, combine the brown sugar, chili powder, salt, cayenne, black pepper, and garlic powder and toss to combine.

In a large bowl, toss the sweet potatoes with the oil, ginger, and half of the spice blend. Evenly spread the potatoes in one single, uncrowded layer on the baking sheet. Bake until the bottom of the wedges are lightly golden brown, 18 to 20 minutes.

Using a metal spatula, gently flip the wedges over to cook the other side. Bake until the potatoes are lightly golden brown on top, 10 to 12 more minutes. While they're still warm, sprinkle them with the remaining spice blend and additional salt to taste.

Fanfare Tip

Ketchup won't cut it here. Need an outrageous dip to pair with these zesty wedges? Swipe them through the Maple Honey Mustard from the Sweet Onion Potato Chip—Crusted Chicken (page 129).

Spicy Israeli Couscous with Toasted Garlic and Hazelnuts

I would eat my sneakers if they were doused in butter, garlic oil, and parmesan—but lucky for me, well, and my sneakers, this wildly addictive side dish calls for Israeli couscous. Thinly shaved toasted garlic and fiery red pepper flakes add a spicy bite to this pearl-shaped pasta, while nutty chopped hazelnuts create a buttery crunch.

1½ cups Israeli couscous	1 tablespoon unsalted butter ★
¼ cup chopped hazelnuts	½ cup grated parmesan cheese
3 tablespoons olive oil	1 teaspoon grated lemon zest
3 medium cloves garlic, thinly sliced	¼ cup chopped fresh parsley
½ teaspoon red pepper flakes	Kosher salt and coarse black pepper

Bring a large pot of salted water to a boil. Add the couscous, cover the pot, and reduce the heat to medium-low. Cook until al dente, 6 to 8 minutes.

In a dry small skillet, toast the hazelnuts over medium-low heat, tossing frequently, until lightly golden and very fragrant, about 5 minutes. Immediately remove the nuts from the pan and transfer to a bowl to stop the cooking process.

★ When I was little, my dad starred in his very own rendition of *Julie & Julia*. He would flip open the splattered pages of *Mastering the Art of French Cooking* and manifest Julia Child masterpieces out of nowhere. The rice soubise—a heavenly casserole of thin-slivered onions, butter, and nutty Gruyère—was as over-the-top delicious as it sounds. This couscous, with toasted garlic, sharp parmesan, and fiery butter, is my grown-up tribute to that savory, gooey side I couldn't get enough of.

In a small skillet, heat the olive oil over medium heat. Add the garlic and pepper flakes. As soon as the garlic turns a light golden brown, 2 to 4 minutes, remove the pan from the heat and stir in the butter.

Drain the couscous and return it to the pot. Add the olive oil and butter mixture, parmesan, hazelnuts, lemon zest, parsley, and ¼ teaspoon each salt and pepper and toss to combine. Adjust the seasoning with salt and pepper.

Fanfare Tips

- To turn this savory vegetarian side into a hearty entrée, grill up a meaty portobello mushroom while the couscous is cooking and slice it over the top.
- Not ready to eat yet? No worries—this simple side is an ideal make-ahead. Prepare the recipe as directed, but stop once you've stirred in the olive oil and butter mixture and the parmesan. Store in the fridge until go-time, reheat on the stove when ready, and stir in the reserved toasted hazelnuts, lemon zest, and parsley just before serving.

White Cheddar and Sage Buttermilk Biscuits

Well, son of a biscuit! Or whatever they say where I'm from. It's time for a sample of the South, y'all. Buttery, flaky biscuits permeated with sharp white cheddar and woody sage make for an ideal side *any* time of the day. Start your morning by stuffing them with a scramble or end your day by using them to mop your dinner plate clean.

2 cups all-purpose flour, sifted

1 tablespoon baking powder

1 tablespoon sugar

1 teaspoon kosher salt

2 tablespoons chopped fresh sage ★

1 cup grated sharp white cheddar cheese

8 tablespoons (1 stick) unsalted butter, frozen

1½ cups buttermilk

Preheat the oven to 450°F.

In a large bowl, mix together the flour, baking powder, sugar, salt, sage, and cheddar. Using a box grater or a food processor with a shredding disc, grate the frozen butter into shreds.

Flippidy-Doo

For an out-of-this-world twist on the First-Prize Breakfast Sandwich with Orange Lavender Fig Jam (page 12), sub these biscuits in for the English muffins.

★ For me, the earthy smell of sage is my time-traveling ticket to a childhood breakfast back home. My dad would slice the fuzzy green leaf into ribbons and mingle it with airy scrambled eggs infused with sharp cheddar. These home-style biscuits permeated with woody sage capture the memory of those delicious, buttery mornings on my parents' oversize purple sofa.

Incorporate the shredded butter into the dry ingredients with a fork until the mixture is coarse and crumbly.

Slowly add 1¼ cups of the buttermilk into the mixture and with your hands, gently knead the dough, being careful not to overmix. Turn the dough out onto a floured surface and pat out 1 inch thick. Using a biscuit cutter or a drinking glass with a 3-inch diameter, begin cutting out biscuits. Once your dough is full of holes, gather the scraps and re-pat them back to the 1-inch thickness. You should end up with 5 biscuits.

Place the biscuits on a nonstick baking sheet and brush the top of each with the remaining ¼ cup buttermilk. Bake until the biscuits are golden and puffy, 12 to 15 minutes.

Fanfare Tip

For a bigger batch of biscuits, use a smaller biscuit cutter or glass. Keep an eye on them in the oven, as the smaller they are, the less time it takes for them to bake.

Garlicky Dill Pickles

Sure, you can buy pickles at the store like everybody else does, but I say: Dare to be different. Right before your eyes—well, if you stare into the fridge for 48 hours—these crunchy cucumber slices transform into crisp, vinegary bites with a mellow garlic flavor and that classic pickle-kick of grassy dill. Slide them into as many sandwiches as possible. Chop them up for homemade Russian dressing. Plop one into your Bloody Mary.

2 cups water

2 cups distilled white vinegar

2 large cloves garlic, gently smashed but still intact

2 tablespoons sugar

2 teaspoons kosher salt

2 teaspoons mustard seeds

2 teaspoons peppercorns (any color)

1½ pounds pickling cucumbers, cut crosswise into ¼-inch-thick rounds

1 small bunch fresh dill

In a large pot, combine the water, vinegar, garlic, sugar, salt, mustard seeds, and peppercorns and bring to a boil.

In an airtight heatproof container, layer the cucumber slices and dill. Pour the boiling liquid over the cucumbers and dill, cover the container with a lid, and refrigerate for 2 to 5 days before using.

Fanfare Tip

Savory pickles not your "bread and butter"? Swap out the dill for an additional ½ cup sugar to satisfy that sweet pickle craving.

Chapter 7

There's Always Room

For me, there's usually room for one more crab cake. Yet still, I have a soft spot for certain sweets. I'm no Betty Crocker, but I am armed with famous brownies and a parfait that will compel you to lick the bowl.

Kailua Coupe with Balsamic Fig Syrup

If you've never been to Hawaii, this treat is your first-class ticket. No sunscreen required. This decadent dessert is stacked with tart sorbet, fresh island fruit, and toasted coconut flakes. Drizzled with a syrupy balsamic fig reduction, every bite is as harmonious as a sun-drenched day on Oahu's Kailua Beach.

¼ cup unsweetened shredded coconut flakes
¼ cup roughly chopped pistachios
1 cup chopped fresh pineapple ★
1 cup chopped mango

Balsamic Fig Syrup (recipe follows)
Several small fresh mint leaves, for garnish
1 pint lemon sorbet (or substitute passion fruit or lime)

Preheat the oven to 350°F.

Spread the coconut flakes onto a small baking sheet and bake, keeping a very close eye as it burns easily, until lightly golden, 2 to 3 minutes.

In a dry small skillet, toast the pistachios over medium-low heat, tossing frequently, until lightly golden and very fragrant, about 5 minutes. Immediately remove the nuts from the pan and transfer to a bowl to stop the cooking process.

In 4 clear, 2-cup coupe glasses or dessert goblets, stack the pineapple, mango, coconut, pistachios, and several of the balsamic-infused figs. Garnish with a light drizzle of the balsamic fig syrup and the mint leaves and then scoop the sorbet over the top.

The year before my sister moved to Hawaii, we visited the tropical utopia and stayed in a resort to celebrate my dad's fiftieth birthday. They had an outdoor breakfast buffet unlike anything I had ever seen. There were gooey, fresh-glazed cinnamon rolls and pancakes covered with macadamia nuts, but nothing was as decadent as the fresh island fruit. I remember pineapple so succulent it melted in my mouth and mangoes so juicy the silky tart segments dissolved onto my tongue.

Balsamic Fig Syrup

MAKES ¼ CUP

½ cup balsamic vinegar
¼ cup stemmed and halved dried black
    mission figs (4 to 6 figs)

In a small pot, combine the vinegar and figs and bring to a simmer over medium-high heat. Reduce the heat to medium-low and cook, stirring occasionally, until thick and syrupy, 6 to 8 minutes.

Fanfare Tip

Sub in different fruits in the coupe for a variety of textures to make your perfect parfait. Kiwi and tart blackberry add a bit of a bite, while chewy bananas keep things smooth and velvety.

Flippidy-Doo

For a sweet and savory crostini, spread toasted baguette slices with creamy, rich Brie and drizzle the balsamic fig syrup over top. Garnish with fresh thyme sprigs for a bright pop of color.

Island-Style Bananas Foster

I agree, Bananas Foster is already pretty perfect. However, I'm a big believer that everything is better in Hawaii. (Wait, put the suitcase down and get back in the kitchen.) For a dessert that will transport your taste buds to the tropics, I bathe bananas and mangoes in a pool of brown sugar and butter, and then tipsy them up with a splash of dark rum. Add a bowl of creamy coconut gelato as the base and you'll be doing the hula in no time.

¼ cup unsweetened shredded coconut
4 tablespoons (½ stick) unsalted butter
¼ cup packed dark brown sugar
Pinch of salt
1 teaspoon pure vanilla extract

2 tablespoons dark rum
4 bananas, ★ cut crosswise on a diagonal into ½-inch-thick slices
1 mango, cut into ½-inch cubes
1 pint coconut gelato

Preheat the oven to 350°F.

Spread the coconut flakes onto a small baking sheet and bake, keeping a very close eye as it burns easily, until lightly golden, 2 to 3 minutes.

In a large skillet, melt the butter over medium heat. Whisk in the brown sugar, salt, and vanilla. When the sugar has completely dissolved, add the rum and increase the heat to medium-high. When the mixture begins to bubble, add the bananas and mango and toss to combine. Sauté until the fruit is thoroughly coated, about 1 minute. Allow to cool to room temperature, about 2 minutes.

Fill 4 bowls with coconut gelato and pour the banana-mango mixture over each one. Garnish with toasted coconut and serve immediately.

Fanfare Tip

For a vegan version of this dessert that embraces all things coconut, swap out the butter for coconut oil and the gelato for coconut milk–based ice cream. It doesn't get much more islandy than that. Well, unless you're wearing your coconut bra.

★ Four years younger than my big sister, I was unexpectedly the brave eater of our family as a kid. My parents were certain that Sarah would never graduate from her fixation with banana yogurt. (Not only did she eventually expand her palate, but she is now a yoga teacher in Hawaii and has a wholesome diet consisting of everything from kale to quinoa.) This banana-centered dessert with a tropical twist is for her.

Mascarpone and Mint Strawberry Cheesecake Pops

MAKES 6 POPSICLES

This velvety lick-on-a-stick is my go-to fix for a cheesecake craving. In this handheld dessert, Italian and American cream cheeses unite. Sweet strawberries, refreshing mint, and tart lime zest mellow out the rich, milky flavors.

1 cup whipped cream cheese, at room temperature

1 cup mascarpone cheese, at room temperature

⅓ cup honey

2 tablespoons finely chopped fresh mint

1 teaspoon pure vanilla extract

¼ teaspoon grated lime zest

Pinch of kosher salt

1 cup diced strawberries

In a large bowl, whisk together the cream cheese, mascarpone, honey, mint, vanilla, lime zest, and salt. Fold in the strawberries and then divide the mixture among six 2-ounce Popsicle molds. Freeze until firm, 4 to 6 hours.

Fanfare Tip

Give this pop some crunch by swirling toasted chopped hazelnuts into the mix.

Sweet Challah Grilled Cheese with Maple, Pear, and Taleggio

SERVES 4

Who says you can't have grilled cheese for dessert? Nobody, that's who. Succulent, eggy sliced challah ain't just for Shabbat anymore, y'all. The sweet braided bread is the crisp, buttery exterior for this salty, sweet, gooey, maple-scented dessert stuffed with tangy Taleggio cheese, juicy pears, and crunchy almonds.

3 tablespoons slivered almonds

4 thick slices challah bread or brioche loaf

5 ounces Taleggio cheese, rind removed and sliced

1 pear, peeled and thinly sliced

2 tablespoons unsalted butter, melted

3 tablespoons maple syrup

In a dry small skillet, toast the slivered almonds over medium-low heat, tossing frequently, until lightly golden and very fragrant, about 5 minutes. Immediately remove the nuts from the pan and transfer to a bowl to stop the cooking process.

Top 2 of the challah slices with the Taleggio, pear, and almonds. Top the sandwiches with another slice of challah. In a small bowl, whisk together the melted butter and 2 tablespoons of the maple syrup and brush half of this mixture on top of both sandwiches.

Heat a large nonstick skillet over medium heat. Lay both sandwiches into the pan butter-side down. Use a heavy pan to weight the sandwiches down as you cook the first side. Cook until the bottoms are lightly golden brown, 2 to 3 minutes.

Brush the tops of the sandwiches with the remaining maple butter and flip the sandwiches over to cook the other side until golden, 1 to 2 minutes.

Cut the sandwiches in half and evenly drizzle them with the remaining 1 tablespoon maple syrup.

Fanfare Tip

To propel these melty treats further into dessertland, trickle warm chocolate-hazelnut spread over the top instead of the additional maple syrup.

Bourbon-Spiked Butterscotch Fondue

Salted caramel is the new butterscotch, but I'm bringing us back to the old school. Not the one where Will Ferrell goes streaking—the one with vanilla. Well, and bourbon of course. Whip up a pot of this warm, buttery, brown sugar–based dessert sauce and break out the skewers.

We're going fondue-ing.

BUTTERSCOTCH SAUCE

4 tablespoons (½ stick) unsalted butter
¼ cup packed light brown sugar
¼ cup packed dark brown sugar
½ teaspoon kosher salt
½ cup heavy cream
1 teaspoon pure vanilla extract
1 tablespoon bourbon

FONDUE

2 bananas, cut crosswise into 1-inch-thick rounds
2 Pink Lady apples, unpeeled and sliced into thin wedges
1 pint strawberries, hulled

Make the butterscotch sauce: In a medium saucepan, melt the butter over low heat. Whisk in both brown sugars and the salt until thoroughly blended, then whisk in the heavy cream. Increase the heat to medium so the mixture comes to a very low boil. Once it boils, cook for 3 minutes, stirring often. Remove the sauce from the heat and whisk in the vanilla and bourbon. Serve while still warm.

For the fondue: Pour the warm butterscotch into a bowl and serve in the middle of a platter with the fruit and toothpicks or skewers for dipping. *Note: The sauce will thicken as it cools.*

Fanfare Tip

Make this a fun-due by breaking out the brews to pair with your butterscotch dip. Go for malty stouts or strong ales like an English-style barley wine to match the vanilla notes in the fondue.

Are You There, Tart? It's Me, Fanny

On my family's annual excursion to my sister's Hawaiian habitat, the visit is never complete without a pilgrimage to our favorite Asian hot spot, Sansei.

It was 2004 and my parents, sister, and I had nearly concluded our first-ever Sansei experience. We sat giddy with joy and high on tuna when dessert menus were offered, and as usual the collective after-dinner response was, "I just want to see what they have." We were hypnotized by the words "homemade warm caramel sauce" and landed on the Granny Smith Apple Tart.

The waitress lowered the plate to the center of the table. The blonde puff pastry sat there modestly for a moment, and then its baked apple and toasted brown sugar perfume began to drift from person to person. The delicate, puffy tart rested in a pool of rich caramel and was topped with a glistening halo of vanilla bean–dotted ice cream. Like vultures with forks, we dismantled and consumed it within seconds.

I had caramel on my elbows. Sarah licked the plate. It was at that moment that the tart joined our family as the grand finale for what would become our yearly Sansei ceremony.

And dessert as we knew it would never be the same.

★ **Vanilla Cardamom Baked Apples** (opposite page): No pastry dough required for these tender baked apples—gooey with brown sugar and dusted with warm, lemony cardamom.

Sarah praying to the apple tart gods.

Vanilla Cardamom Baked Apples

A wise woman once said, "How easy was that?" That woman was Ina Garten—and she was right. Some of the best dishes begin and end with simplicity. When you're itching to indulge without all the fuss, reach for an apple, some ice cream, and a few pantry staples for a gooey, caramelized treat enhanced by warm, peppery cardamom.

It will be the easiest dessert you'll ever make.

Or breakfast.

Hey, I'm not judging.

4 Pink Lady apples, peeled and thinly sliced
1 teaspoon ground cardamom
Pinch of kosher salt

½ cup packed dark brown sugar
1 tablespoon pure vanilla extract
4 cups cinnamon-flavored ice cream

Preheat the oven to 375°F.

In a large bowl, toss the apples with the cardamom and salt. Divide into 4 portions and place each onto a piece of foil large enough to wrap up the apples. Divide the brown sugar and vanilla evenly among the portions and seal the foil so that the apples are enclosed.

Place the packages on a baking sheet and bake until the apples are soft and gooey, 30 to 35 minutes depending on their size.

Pour each portion of baked apples and all of their sauce into a bowl. Scoop the cinnamon ice cream over top.

Fanfare Tip

For a decadent breakfast, bake these spiced apples the night before and stir them into your oatmeal the next morning.

Flippidy-Doo

For a shortcut to a flaky apple tart, break out the muffin tin and mold 2-inch squares of store-bought puff pastry into the cups. Poke the dough with a fork to keep it from rising and bake until golden. Spoon the warm sugary apples into the crispy shells. If you're feeling especially wild, finish them with a spoonful of Bourbon-Spiked Butterscotch Fondue (page 203).

The Brownie Legacy

This is a story about a famous brownie.

A brownie that flew on airplanes, was a guest on *The Phil Donahue Show*, and once granted me lunch with the president. Although I was several months from being born, technically Ronald Reagan and I shared roast beef that day. This is the story about the legendary Rachel's Brownies—better yet, this is a story about my mom.

Just out of college in summer 1975, my mom was exploring new avenues for her creativity as her dreams of being a concert pianist were unexpectedly side-lined. To earn a little money, she began to bake and sell decadently rich, double-chocolate brownies to several gourmet stores in Philadelphia. Nine months later, these homemade masterpieces were declared "best in the city" by *Philadelphia* magazine and became an overnight sensation. It was as if my mom's artistic tem-perament had transformed mere chocolate into food for the gods. Over the next few years the business achieved cult status, but it grew slowly under my mom's perfectionist stewardship.

In 1978, a year after their marriage, my parents began to operate as a team. My dad's extraordinary sales and marketing skills blended with my mom's artistry and passion for excellence, and the rest is history. They created an enormously successful, nationally acclaimed business—built on love, marketing, and choco-late chips—that would live on for decades. They created a craze in Häagen-Dazs stores and gourmet shops across the country. They were ordered by Henry Fonda's wife for his seventy-fifth birthday party.

But for me, these gooey, fudgy morsels were simply a part of our family. To this day, I often make the butterscotch version—known as Rachel's Husband's Brownies—when I'm feeling a bit homesick. I can't help but indulge in the caramel-scented, salty batter, as il brings me back to my three-year-old self. It's as if I'm licking a spatula that has traveled through time. At that age, I was completely unaware of the brownies' fame outside of our family kitchen. To me, they were simply a blissful bite of home.

They were the scrumptious, chewy chocolate mouthfuls my sister and I devoured with cold milk as my mom handed us sinfully moist brownies still warm from the oven. They were the frozen, butterscotch-laced late-night snack—deliciously chilled, blaring with rich brown sugar and chocolate chips. They were the *tap-tap-tap* of the buttered 9 x 13 pan against my dad's palm as a cloud of flour skated across the glossy dish from corner to corner.

In an interview my mom was once quoted as saying, "We must always remember that the single most important thing about our business is not our balance sheet or profit and loss statement. It is the singularly magnificent taste of our brownies themselves—their richness and sheer decadence."

My mom was in her twenties when she began her own successful food busi-

1977. Mom, age twenty-five, preparing to bake dozens of her homemade double-chocolate brownies to sell to gourmet food shops in Philadelphia.

1984. My parents making brownie magic in their Malvern, Pennsylvania, bakery. I made my entry onto the scene the following year as their newest product.

ness in the kitchen, and as fate would have it, I happen to be walking down a parallel path. Perhaps a piece of my guiding light is the rare soul of Rachel's Brownies—blooming inside me like a fresh pan of brownies and inspiring my hunger every step of the way.

★ **Rachel's Daughter's French Roast Brownies** (opposite page): Rachel's Husband's Brownies, my dad's play on the original creation, have always inspired me to invent a Rachel's Brownie flavor of my very own. These mocha-tinged sweets swimming with dark, smoky French roast are an ode to my parents. They are a symphony of lush deep chocolate and bold coffee—a true fusion of my mom and dad.

Rachel's Daughter's French Roast Brownies

MAKES 20 BROWNIES

Many of us cooks out there also happen to be avid nonbakers. We don't own measuring cups and prefer to season in pinches and handfuls. I'm with you on that one, but trust me that these brownies are foolproof. A double dose of chocolate gives these gooey sweets irresistible decadence, and smoky, intense French roast coffee adds a mellow mocha undertone.

½ cup ground French roast coffee
¾ cup water
2 sticks (½ pound) unsalted butter
4 ounces unsweetened chocolate, chopped
4 large eggs

2¼ cups sugar
2 teaspoons pure vanilla extract
¾ cup all-purpose flour, sifted
½ teaspoon baking powder
½ teaspoon kosher salt
6 ounces semisweet chocolate chips

Preheat the oven to 335°F. Grease and flour a 9 x 13-inch baking pan.

In a coffeemaker, brew the coffee grounds with the water to make very strong coffee. You should have ½ cup. Set it aside.

In a small saucepan, combine the butter and chocolate and whisk over low heat until thoroughly combined and melted. Set aside to cool.

In a large bowl, with an electric mixer, beat the eggs and sugar together until thick. Beat in the vanilla. Slowly beat in the chocolate and butter mixture, then the brewed coffee.

In a small bowl, stir together the flour, baking powder, and salt. With the mixer on low, slowly blend the flour mixture into the batter. With the mixer still running, mix in the chocolate chips.

Pour the batter into the pan and bake until a toothpick comes out clean, 30 to 35 minutes. The center should still be a bit loose and the outside edges should be set. Let the brownies cool completely in the pan before cutting into 20 brownies.

Fanfare Tip

Although it's hard to beat warm, fresh-out-of-the-oven brownies, pop one of these treats into the freezer for a chewy, chocolaty midnight snack.

Frozen No Bakes with Peanut Butter and Honey

When it comes to chicken, the oven is my friend. If we're talking cookies . . . I'm a no-bake kind of girl. Also, it's somehow less shameful to eat batter that you don't *actually* have to bake. These sweet treats are taken to the next level with peanut butter and a syrupy drizzle of honey. No-bake cookies can have a tendency to be runny, so I borrow a little help from the freezer.

Go on, eat the batter. No one's looking.

1½ cups sugar
6 tablespoons unsalted butter
⅔ cup milk
¾ cup creamy peanut butter (avoid using all-natural peanut butter as it separates)

⅛ teaspoon ground cinnamon
½ teaspoon pure vanilla extract
2 cups quick-cooking oats
2 tablespoons honey, for drizzling

Grease a baking sheet and clear room for it in your freezer.

In a small saucepan, combine the sugar, butter, and ⅓ cup of the milk. Bring to a boil over medium-high heat and boil for exactly 1 minute, then remove the pan from the heat. Whisk in the peanut butter, cinnamon, and vanilla. Transfer the mixture to a large bowl and stir in the oats. The batter may be a bit crumbly, so add several tablespoons of milk at a time to remoisten it. It should be wet but not overly saturated.

Using ¼ cup of batter at a time, drop the cookies onto the baking sheet and place the pan in the freezer. Once the cookies are firm, about 45 minutes, drizzle them with the honey. Store in the freezer.

Flippidy-Doo

For a toasty flavor on these frozen treats, sprinkle them with the coconut dust from Coconut-Kissed Calamari with Lime-Agave Dip (page 100).

Chapter 8

Awesomesauce

Some like it hot. I like it saucy. In this chapter I teach you to turn up the volume on mundane plates with the simple addition of an extraordinary sauce. Flavor-packed pestos, jams, aiolis, and so on are an outstanding way to decorate any dish.

Kale and Toasted Pistachio Pesto

Pesto is kind of like that fast-food chain that says "Have it your way"—except there's no creepily masked mascot in a pimp robe. Swap out ingredients as you like to produce *your* perfect pesto. For me, I like to pack in nutrients wherever I can. The herby green sauce in this recipe gets a punch of vitamin K from one of my favorite super-veggies: kale. Toasted pistachios intensify the vibrancy in the already emerald-shaded sauce.

¼ cup pistachios
1 medium clove garlic
Kosher salt and coarse black pepper
¼ cup grated parmesan cheese
1½ cups roughly chopped kale leaves
 (a tender variety such as lacinato),
 ribs removed

½ cup packed fresh basil leaves
Juice of 1 lemon
1 teaspoon honey
⅓ to ½ cup olive oil

In a dry small skillet, toast the pistachios over medium-low heat, tossing frequently, until lightly golden and very fragrant, about 5 minutes. Immediately remove the nuts from the pan and transfer to a bowl to stop the cooking process.

In a food processor, combine the toasted pistachios, garlic, and a generous pinch each of salt and pepper. Pulse a few times until the nuts are broken down. Add the parmesan, kale, basil, lemon juice, and honey and pulse until the mixture is thoroughly combined. With the motor running, stream in ⅓ cup of the olive oil. If the mixture is too chunky, add a bit more oil. For a thinner pesto, continue adding oil until the consistency is velvety and smooth. Season to taste with salt and pepper.

Fanfare Tip

How do I love pesto? Let me count the ways. On an English muffin with a fluffy scrambled egg. Whisked into butter for a dipping sauce with shrimp. Stirred into angel hair. Spread onto a grilled cheese with sharp cheddar.

Rosemary Roasted Scallion Pesto

I believe in love. And by love, I mean scallions.

These young onions are underrated and underused. Yes, I know you sprinkle them onto your baked potato, and I don't care. Follow me to the oven for a green onion game changer. A quick roast leaves these stalks caramelized and cooing with charred flavor. A food processor, some woody rosemary, and a few pulses later you've got a prestigious pesto you can't find on any grocery store shelf.

2 small bunches thick scallions, trimmed but whole
1 tablespoon olive oil
Kosher salt and coarse black pepper
¼ cup unsalted raw sunflower seeds
1 medium clove garlic
¼ cup grated parmesan cheese

3 tablespoons roughly chopped fresh rosemary
½ cup packed fresh basil leaves
¼ cup fresh lemon juice
2 teaspoons honey
⅔ to 1 cup olive oil

Preheat the oven to 400°F.

On a baking sheet, drizzle the scallions with the olive oil and sprinkle with salt and pepper. Roast until the scallions are golden and caramelized, 18 to 20 minutes.

In a dry small skillet, toast the sunflower seeds over medium-low heat, tossing frequently, until lightly golden and very fragrant, about 5 minutes. Immediately remove the seeds from the pan and transfer to a bowl to stop the cooking process.

In a food processor, combine the roasted scallions, sunflower seeds, garlic, and a pinch each of salt and pepper and pulse a few times until the seeds are broken down. Add the parmesan, rosemary, basil, lemon juice, and honey. Pulse until the mixture is thoroughly combined.

With the motor running, slowly stream in ⅔ cup of the olive oil. If the pesto is still a bit chunky, add the remaining oil to make it smooth. Season to taste with salt and pepper.

Fanfare Tips

- When the warm weather hits, keep an eye out at your local market for spring onions. Swap them in for scallions and you'll get a mellow pesto with a sweeter bite.
- Make a double batch and freeze the rest in an ice cube tray. Need a quick weeknight dinner? Pop a cube out and swirl it into melted butter for an herby sauce to shower over seared fish.

The Right Stuff

There is no cooler person in the world to me than my big sister, Sarah.

When I was four, I would follow her and her friends around like a stage five clinger. I meant no harm, I was simply hoping they would teach me their ways—namely side ponytails and their meticulous choreography for New Kids on the Block's "The Right Stuff." At some point circa 1995, Sarah became smitten with sunflower seeds. Eating them was her absolute favorite summer pastime, other than attempting to beat her personal record on the Skip-it. She would carry a crinkly plastic tube of these salty snacks around, crunching and spitting like a pro. She adored their addictive nutty flavor and crispy texture and was rarely without an open bag.

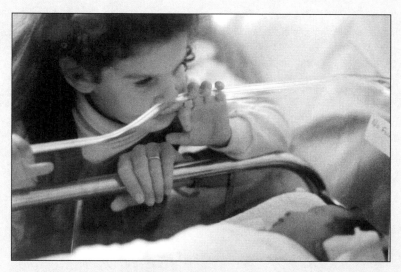

Sarah, age four, taking her first day on the job as big sister very seriously. She would go on to mentor me in the art of New Kids on the Block choreography and summertime snacking.

It was a humid North Carolina summer day and Sarah was in our living room, ear pressed to a boom box memorizing the words to Paula Abdul's newest hit. I tiptoed into her room and snagged several seeds from the half-empty package on her bed. Sitting cross-legged on my floor, I began to fling the teardrop shapes into my mouth. Unaware that the dark shells were inedible and the real treat was hidden inside, I spent what felt like an hour chomping away with no surrender. When I finally grew bored, I pursed my lips and deeply inhaled a gulp of air. With one whooshing breath back out, 600 bits and pieces of sunflower seeds and shells were strewn about my room. They stuck to the carpet and speckled the nearest Persian cat.

Yep, I thought, *I am definitely not as cool as my sister.*

Many years later, I schooled myself on the wonders of these nutritious kernels, and now I slip them into my dishes wherever possible.

★ **Sunflower Seed–Cream Cheese Pesto** (page 216) on **Roasted Veggie Crostini** (page 78): I've created a smooth, nut-free spread packed with these wholesome seeds. The cream cheese adds a rich, full-bodied flavor to the pesto and makes a wonderful contrast to the smoky roasted vegetables on the crostini.

Sunflower Seed–Cream Cheese Pesto

Cream cheese and pesto in the same sentence? Don't worry, you're not dreaming. The name may *sound* fancy, but just a few buzzes of the food processor and you're on your way to whipping up this savory spreadable sauce filled with fluffy cream cheese and tart lemon.

¼ cup unsalted raw sunflower seeds
2 small cloves garlic
Kosher salt and coarse black pepper
¼ cup grated parmesan cheese
1½ cups packed fresh basil leaves

1 teaspoon honey
Juice of 1 lemon
½ cup olive oil
½ cup whipped cream cheese

In a dry small skillet, toast the sunflower seeds over medium-low heat, tossing frequently, until lightly golden and very fragrant, about 5 minutes. Immediately remove the seeds from the pan and transfer to a bowl to stop the cooking process.

In a food processor, pulse the sunflower seeds, garlic, and a generous pinch each of salt and pepper until the seeds are broken down. Add the parmesan, basil, honey, and lemon juice and pulse until thoroughly combined. With the motor running, stream in the olive oil a little bit at a time until the pesto is velvety.

Add the cream cheese to the food processor and pulse until the pesto is very creamy and smooth. Season to taste with salt and pepper.

Fanfare Tips

- This spreadable sauce ain't just for spreadin'. Toss it with al dente elbow noodles and sharp cheddar, pour into a soup crock, top with parmesan, and bake until golden for the mack daddy of mac and cheese.
- Sunflower seeds are the perfect substitute for pricey pine nuts—which typically go in pesto. They also work as a fantastic variation for those with nut allergies. Can't find sunflower seeds? Roasted unsalted pumpkin seeds work like a charm.

Orange Lavender Fig Jam

Today could be the day that you pat yourself on the back and congratulate yourself for making fig jam. I'm very proud of you. This fragrant, juicy spread can do no wrong, and there's nowhere it can't go. Try it on crackers, on toast, in a wrap. Try it in a box, with a fox, with a mouse, in a house.

Wait, I got carried away.

Just try it. Trust me.

1 pound fresh figs, stemmed and halved (or ½ pound dried figs, stemmed)
1 teaspoon grated orange zest
3 tablespoons orange juice (or ½ cup if using dried figs)

⅓ cup packed light brown sugar (or ¼ cup if using dried figs)
½ tablespoon fresh lavender ★ or 1 teaspoon dried
Pinch of kosher salt

In a medium saucepan, combine the figs, orange zest, orange juice, brown sugar, lavender, and salt. Bring to a boil over medium-high heat. If using fresh figs, mash with a potato masher. Reduce the heat to medium-low and simmer for 10 minutes. If using dried figs, now you can mash with a potato masher or pulse in a food processor for a very smooth spread. Refrigerate the jam for at least 20 minutes before serving.

Fanfare Tip

Make entertaining easy on yourself. A few elegant crackers, several varieties of artisanal cheese (Saint André, Drunken Goat, English Stilton), and a bowl of this fig jam will win you hostess of the year in a pinch—of lavender.

★ Growing up with a certified energy healer for a mom meant that in our house, essential oils were as common as spice rubs. When I've succumbed to stress, the sweet, floral aroma of lavender cradles me like the therapeutic arms of my mom. I incorporate the calming herb wherever I can, as its soothing flavor further enhances an already harmonious treat like fig jam.

For the Love of Figs

Hi, my name is Fanny, and I love figs.

Why do I love figs so much, you ask? Well, that's the type of question that ultimately doesn't require an answer, like "Where do babies come from?" or "Whatever happened to Pee-wee Herman?" What matters is that despite my adoration of countless ingredients, I've always been searching for the one. The one that resonates on a deeper level. The one that lights up my soul. The one that feels less like a component in a dish, and more like a sidekick.

To my faithful cat, Olive, yes, you are my actual sidekick—but I don't think that drizzling you with honey and pairing you with semisoft cheeses would be ideal for your fur.

This eccentric, fruity infatuation came later in life when I stumbled upon a fresh fig for the very first time in my twenties. My coastal town had finally hopped on the Whole Foods train, and I considered hauling my queen-size bed into their soon-to-be parking lot. It's not like the first hundred customers got to ride the grass-fed beef or anything, but I wanted the privilege of being there on opening day and, more important, first dibs on the cheese samples. I burst through the automatic doors and landed in their vibrant produce department.

The abundant market was so packed with eager-eyed patrons hustling their way to the local parsnips that I nearly took shelter under the apricots for safety. I pressed my basket to my chest and slipped through the zealous crowd. When the sea of shoppers finally cleared, a colorful display ahead caught my eye. I took a few steps forward and looked down. I was face-to-fruit with my very first fresh fig. There were infinite rows of deep purple, Granny-Smith-green, and glowing magenta. These tiny masterpieces stood straight up like chubby little soldiers with their pointy heads and plump bodies. I quietly nodded hello.

In a matter of minutes I was home and slicing through juicy Black Mission figs. They split open to reveal glossy, bright burgundy flesh inside, and I piled them into a bowl. How was I to know that the wrinkly, plum-colored, bell-shaped fruits I had familiarized myself with as figs *stemmed* from such beauty? I spread them onto crackers, scattered them throughout my recipes, my catering business, and my life. I was no Girl & the Fig, but I was gifted that very cookbook by my parents, and I found solace in the fact that I was not alone in my craving.

★ **Balsamic Fig Jam** (page 220): In this jam, I've permeated my beloved figs—the juicy fresh variety and the sugary dried capsules—with acidic, syrupy balsamic. The thick sweetness of the honey offsets the bold vinegar to create a perfectly balanced spread.

★ **Fig and Brie Frittata with Caramelized Leeks** (page 28): This fluffy favorite plucks the fruit from the tree and drops it into some eggs with buttery Brie and fresh mint.

My very first fig tree, Newton. He was stolen from my front yard after just four months and never got to celebrate his Jam Mitzvah. I'm still pissed about it.

Balsamic Fig Jam

Balsamic and figs are the Bert and Ernie of your pantry. Other than the unibrow, they're pretty much the exact same thing. They do okay apart, but ultimately belong together. Fig jam by itself is delightful—but splash in some sharp balsamic and the world just makes sense. This savory jam pairs beautifully with tangy chèvre and makes a grilled cheese so good it's illegal in 25 states.

1 pound fresh figs, stemmed and halved (or ½ pound dried figs, stemmed)

¼ cup balsamic vinegar (or ½ cup if using dried figs)

2 tablespoons honey

1 tablespoon fresh lemon juice

Pinch of kosher salt

In a medium saucepan, combine the figs, balsamic (plus ¼ cup water if using dried figs), honey, lemon juice, and salt. Bring to a boil over medium-high heat. If using fresh figs, mash with a potato masher. Reduce the heat to medium-low and simmer for 10 minutes. If using dried figs, now you can mash with a potato masher or pulse in a food processor. Refrigerate the jam for at least 20 minutes before serving.

Fanfare Tip

How to throw a casual modern dinner party with elegant style? Serve down-to-earth fare like cheeseburgers and elevate them with a touch of class. Dab a spoonful of balsamic fig jam onto each patty for a sharp, sweet unexpected burst of flavor. Melt on Gorgonzola for a tangy contrast.

Whiskey Bacon Jam

If the words "bacon" and "jam" together seem odd to you, well, close this book and walk away. This sinful spread is a trio of caramelized onions, unctuous salty bacon, and sweet Irish whiskey. Smear it onto baguette slices for a BLT Crostini (page 79) or eat it quietly with a spoon late at night when no one can judge you.

12 ounces bacon, ★ roughly chopped
1 medium sweet onion, diced
2 tablespoons dark brown sugar

¼ teaspoon coarse black pepper
½ cup sweet Irish whiskey, such as Jameson

In a medium saucepan, heat the chopped bacon over medium heat and cook until lightly crisp, 15 to 20 minutes. Remove it with a slotted spoon and set aside on paper towels to drain.

To the bacon fat, add the onion, brown sugar, and pepper and simmer until the onion is very translucent, about 5 minutes.

Add the whiskey, increase the heat to high, and bring to a boil. Reduce the heat to low, return the bacon to the pan, and simmer, stirring occasionally, until the jam is a rich brown color, 30 to 35 minutes.

Using an immersion blender (or transferring the mixture to a food processor), pulse several times until the consistency is spreadable but still slightly chunky.

Flippidy-Doo

For a truly outrageous BLT breakfast twist—slather this jam onto your Open-Faced Scramble Sandwich with Roasted Tomato Butter (page 32)—it's okay, butter and bacon are BFFs.

Fanfare Tip

Split the batch into three, swap out the Irish whiskey for local bourbon, and hold a bourbon bacon jam tasting this weekend. (Can I come?)

★ As a kid, I once told my grandmother Bea I liked bacon. Over the next twenty years of visits to her home, she was always armed for my arrival with infinite packages of pork. Although two or three of the salty strips would have sufficed, she would stand by the microwave in her robe until every last piece was crisped to perfection. If love were measured in bacon, Bea Bea could put Oscar Mayer out of business. The sizzling, smoky aroma of this bacon jam will forever whisk me back to those savory Springfield, New Jersey, mornings by her side.

Grilled Pineapple Aioli

Scoot over, chicken kebabs—give the fruit a turn. This sweet and savory aioli begins by collecting unicorns from a field. Just kidding, but it is *that* ridiculously good. Juicy pineapple and fresh lemon are seared on the grill until caramelized, and then thick Greek yogurt and mayonnaise bring the fruity sauce to a smooth finish.

Drizzle onto fish tacos for dinner or into your mouth just for fun.

1 tablespoon olive oil
½ lemon
⅓ pineapple, peeled, cored, and cut into ½-inch-thick rings (about 8 ounces)

¼ cup plain Greek yogurt
¼ cup champagne vinegar
2 tablespoons mayonnaise
Kosher salt and coarse black pepper

Preheat a grill or grill pan to medium-high.

Brush the olive oil onto the lemon half and pineapple rings. Grill the lemon flesh-side down until charred, about 3 minutes. Grill the pineapple 3 to 5 minutes per side until caramelized. Cool to room temperature and roughly chop.

In a blender, combine the chopped pineapple, yogurt, vinegar, and mayonnaise. Squeeze in the juice from the charred lemon. Pulse until very smooth. Season to taste with salt and pepper.

Fanfare Tip

Fruit is naturally sweet, so caramelizing it on the grill heightens and enhances its already delicious flavor. Opt for fresh varieties that will hold up to the heat—like peaches, nectarines, and apricots—for some delicious variations on this decadent aioli.

Flippidy-Doo

The sugary flavors in this spread make it an excellent swap-in for the honey drizzle that balances out the salt in Parmesan-Crusted Prosciutto and White Cheddar Wraps (page 58).

Roasted Tomato Aioli

I would take the savory scent of aromatics caramelizing away in the oven over perfume *any day*. In this all-purpose aioli, nutty garlic, sweet shallot, and acidic tomatoes are roasted until golden and rich and pulsed with creamy Greek yogurt and tart lime for a tangy, toma-toey spread.

3 vine-ripened or Roma (plum) tomatoes, halved
1 small shallot, halved
1 medium clove garlic, peeled
1 tablespoon olive oil

Kosher salt and coarse black pepper
¼ cup plain Greek yogurt
2 tablespoons mayonnaise
1 tablespoon fresh lime juice
½ teaspoon honey

Preheat the oven to 400°F.

In a baking dish, toss the tomatoes, shallot, and garlic with the oil and season generously with salt and pepper. Roast until the garlic clove is golden and the tomatoes are broken down, 18 to 20 minutes. Cool to room temperature.

In a blender, pulse the cooled tomato mixture with the yogurt, mayonnaise, lime juice, and honey until very smooth. Season to taste with salt and pepper.

Fanfare Tip

This versatile sauce has a place at the breakfast, lunch, or dinner table. Drizzle over poached eggs as an alternative to hollandaise, spread between sourdough slices for a zesty turkey sandwich, or dollop onto crab cakes for dinner.

Gorgonzola Tzatziki

To those who fear blue cheese, please don't turn the page. I promise it's not as scary as it seems. I use Gorgonzola dolce here—the sweeter, milder younger cousin of blue cheese. This tasty tzatziki blends thick Greek yogurt, floral mint, and lemony dill. The creamy, re-freshing combination will remind you of a slightly funkier version of ranch.

Play that funky dip, homeboy.

¼ cup grated peeled seedless cucumber (grated on the large holes of a box grater)
Kosher salt and coarse black pepper
1 cup plain Greek yogurt

3 ounces Gorgonzola dolce, crumbled
1 tablespoon chopped fresh dill
1 tablespoon chopped fresh mint
2 small cloves garlic ★, finely minced
2 tablespoons fresh lemon juice

Place the grated cucumber in a colander set in the sink and generously sprinkle with salt. Toss and let sit for at least 20 minutes. Place the cucumber in cheesecloth or a clean kitchen towel and squeeze out the excess water.

In a large bowl, combine the cucumber, yo-gurt, Gorgonzola, dill, mint, garlic, and lemon juice. Thoroughly whisk the sauce so that the Gorgonzola blends in. Season to taste with salt and pepper.

Fanfare Tip

This spread isn't just for dolloping on homemade Baked Veggie Falafel (page 74). Surround it with sliced veggies and use it as a substitute for traditional ranch dip. So good you don't want to share it? Wrap it up inside a whole wheat tortilla with turkey, avocado, and mixed greens for a healthy weekday lunch.

★ Each week my mom would return home from an afternoon of errands with an array of treats from our favorite specialty food shop. I would bury my head in the brown paper bag, tossing aside croissants and chocolate chip cookies. It was the creamy, herbaceous vege-table dip ignited by pungent garlic that I had my eye on. This sensationally zesty spread is the addictive inspiration for this tangy tzatziki.

Roasted Garlic

Dear generic flowery scented air freshener, you've been replaced. Nothing fills a home with comfort better than the smell of garlic. So simple a monkey could do it: Roasted garlic is one of the most straightforward ingredients you, or your pet monkey, has ever prepared. As the cloves roast they become mellow, nutty, sweet, and spreadable.

1 head garlic

½ teaspoon olive oil

Pinch of kosher salt

Preheat the oven to 400°F.

Slice off the very top of the garlic head so that the cloves are exposed. Drizzle the cloves with the oil and sprinkle with the salt. Wrap the entire head in foil and bake until golden and tender, 50 to 55 minutes.

To pop out the cloves, gently squeeze them out of their shells.

Fanfare Tips

- A big golden head of roasted garlic makes a gorgeous addition to a gourmet cheese and fruit plate. Serve with a butter knife and crusty bread.
- To add richness to soups and sauces, mash the garlic cloves with the flat side of your knife and stir them in. The paste will dissolve perfectly into the warm liquid.
- To mix the mashed cloves into a room temperature substance, like a vinaigrette, use a blender or food processor to scatter them evenly throughout.

Spicy Guava Butter

Sweet, exotic guava nectar and spicy cayenne are whisked into velvety, buttery bliss in this 10-minute sauce. There's really not much this tropical butter infusion *isn't* good on. Fish, chicken, veggies, your face.

Go on, you deserve it.

1½ cups guava nectar
3 tablespoons apricot jam
1½ tablespoons honey
1 teaspoon cayenne pepper

Kosher salt
4 tablespoons (½ stick) unsalted butter, softened

In a small saucepan, whisk together the guava nectar, apricot jam, honey, cayenne, and a pinch of salt. Bring the mixture to a low boil over medium-high heat. Reduce the heat to medium and simmer, stirring occasionally, until the mixture has thickened and reduced by about one-third, 8 to 10 minutes. Remove the pan from the heat and whisk in the butter. Season to taste with salt.

Fanfare Tip

In Hawaii, appetizers are called "pupus." For a quick island-worthy pupu, grill up some shrimp and pineapple skewers and slather on this spicy sauce. Speaking of pupu, to cut your time in the kitchen, opt for already deveined shrimp.

Basil Marinara

I'm no Italian grandmother, but I certainly do enjoy standing over a simmering pot of marinara. This vibrant sauce works fantastic as a base—try swirling in some vodka and heavy cream—or stands beautifully all by itself. Torn sweet basil brings a light, floral note, and earthy dried oregano adds that undeniably Italian flavor. Everyone should have a go-to marinara under their belt—or on top of their pasta.

Hey, where you choose to put it is your business.

1 cup packed fresh basil leaves
2 tablespoons olive oil
1 large shallot, minced
2 medium cloves garlic, minced
1 teaspoon dried oregano

Pinch of red pepper flakes
Kosher salt and coarse black pepper
1 tablespoon tomato paste
2 cans (28 ounces each) crushed tomatoes
1 teaspoon sugar

Roughly chop half of the basil leaves and gently tear the other half.

In a large saucepan, heat the olive oil over medium heat. Add the shallot, garlic, oregano, pepper flakes, ½ teaspoon salt, and ¼ teaspoon black pepper and cook until very fragrant, about 2 minutes. Whisk in the tomato paste and cook for 30 seconds. Add both cans of tomatoes, the chopped basil, and the sugar and stir well to combine. Cover the pot and simmer, stirring occasionally, over medium-low heat for at least 30 minutes and preferably 1 hour.

Just before serving, stir in the remaining torn basil and season to taste with salt and pepper.

Fanfare Tips

- When the warm weather hits and the farmers' markets are in full bloom, snatch up some local heirloom tomatoes. Roughly chop and substitute them in for one of the cans of tomatoes.
- Freeze half of the batch so you'll have a summery sauce on hand for months.

Acknowledgments

I'd like to take this page to raise my glass to the recipe of extraordinary individuals who have transformed my cookbook dream into a reality.

While this book is dedicated to the three members of my immediate family, it also very much belongs to the infinitely remarkable Rachael Ray. Her decision to conduct a competition that resulted in a published cookbook opened up a colossal door of opportunity to the world. I just happened to be waiting on the other side. I believe with every fiber of my being that the stars aligned to connect me with Rachael—as I have looked up to her for many more years than she knows. During college, I would sit on the floor in front of the TV and recite the intro to *30 Minute Meals* along with her. I once waited eight hours in line at a bookstore for her to sign my copy of *Just in Time!* She touched my life through the screen—an ability that I could only hope to manifest someday. I wished that even a small fraction of the magic that she spread was inside of me, too. Now under her guidance, I feel as if the world is at my fingertips and I couldn't be more grateful. So thanks, Rach. Thank you for seeing something in me. Thank you for the winks, the reassuring shoulder squeezes, and for allowing me to be exactly who I am. Thank you for being my Oprah. Thank you for opening this door for me. I guarantee it'll be a good show on the other side.

To each and every team member at *The Rachael Ray Show*, I can't thank you enough for making me feel right at home from the beginning. You've laughed at my jokes, you've smiled from across the studio, and you've stocked your pockets with granola bars to postpone my low blood sugar. You make me feel like a part of your family, and I am so lucky to know you all.

Countless thank-yous to all the magnificent individuals at Atria—especially the following: Judith Curr for sharing your desire to live in my kitchen when we met. I instantly felt welcomed into the Atria circle. Immense gratitude to my editor, Johanna Castillo, for celebrating me and this cookbook from our very first conversation (except that time you dressed me up in your high heels during the cover shoot and asked if I would wear pink). Thank you to Kaitlyn Zafonte and Lindsay Newton for cheering me on and guiding me through this incredible experience. Thank you to my art director, Albert Tang, for understanding the soul of my style from the minute you walked onto set, and for pouring me that extra glass of Crown Royal when Johanna made me wear heels. Thank you to my tremendously talented photographer, Frances Janisch, who, with a single click, captured the spirit of me and my food like we were lifelong friends. Thank you, also, for the aforementioned whiskey and for blaring Britney Spears while I posed for the cover. To Frances's assistant, Jody Kivort—thank you for your hard work and unshakable patience as we studied each shot making sure that no fig was out of place. To my food stylist, Hadas Smirnoff: I am so grateful for your seasoned culinary skills and sensational kitchen instincts, which turned my recipes into true works of art. You brought the imagination inside my cookbook to life. Big shout-out to Kate Schmidt, Hadas's assistant, who nailed a perfect sear every time. To my brilliant project editor, Kate Slate—who, in our initial meeting, put me immediately at ease with the reassurance that yes, we are somehow related. Your knack for understanding "Fanny-speak" is unparalleled, and every question you instantly answered and piece of advice you promptly zipped back helped to shape me into a better author. You even, on your own time, joined me in my very first cookbook photo shoot so that there would be a familiar face in the room. How lucky I am to have you as a leader, a professional confidante, and a friend. You are my fairy cookbook godmother.

To everyone at the Atria Publishing Group, thank you for allowing me this journey. I promise to make you all very proud.

To my parents, who have cheered me on through each and every step of life. Thank you, Mom, for praising my silliness and stirring my love for healthy, wholesome foods. Thank you for nurturing and nourishing me, and for helping to pilot me toward my true self. I am inspired by your tremendous strength daily and am so proud that we get to spend this lifetime together—skipping around with chard and offering a round of applause to the cherry tomatoes. Daddy-o, for scooting a chair up to the stove and allowing a four-year-old to sprinkle fresh sage all over your kitchen—thank you for changing my life. Thank you for championing me in every sense of the word. Under your unconditional love and culinary guidance, I have finally found myself—and my third circle. You never stopped believing that eventually, all of this would pay off, and for that, I am eternally grateful. Someday, I will buy you that giraffe for the backyard that you've always wanted. To my big sister, Sar, apparently siblings are supposed to fight . . . but we never got that memo. From the moment my spaceship delivered me to this world, you have been the third caretaker. As the older sister, you have gone above and beyond your job to help me feel protected, cherished, and appreciated. No matter how many states physically stand between us, our love and laughter will always bring us back home. Preferably to a freezer full of brownies and an oven full of crab cakes.

To my extended family scattered throughout New Jersey, I am endlessly appreciative of your undying support. You are all so special to me, and our food adventures together have fostered the frame of this cookbook and ultimately, my life. Thank you for always seeing the star in me and for showering me with so much love. Thank you for being my family. To my incomparable grandmother—Bea Bea, thank you for texting me on November 21, 2013, to let me know that Rachael Ray was holding a cookbook competition. That certainly turned out well. You mean the world to me, and I am so lucky to have shared every moment of this with you. I am so thankful that your Springfield home is just under an hour from New York City—because each time work brings me back north I'm granted one more visit with you. *You* are my winning lottery ticket. I know that Poppy, Aunt Annette, Poppa George, Grandma Fannie, and Aunt Sara have been with us every step of the way.

To Tony, my eager, easy-to-please taste tester and the heart of my support system. Thank you for holding my hand through every page of this book. For eating 10:00 p.m. dinners without an ounce of protest. For always doing the dishes. For always leaving encouraging, handwritten notes in my suitcase. For always trying to get me to dance when I'm mad. For talking me down from frantic rants of stress and hunger. For laughing at my inexplicably fuzzy hair at the end of a fourteen-hour writing day—instead of running in the other direction. I am so lucky to have found my other half. I love you, and yes, I will autograph this book for you.

To my other Sar, what a blessing it is for two friends to find each other in a world full of people. Like the great Carrie Bradshaw once said, "Today I had a thought. What if I had never met you?" You have been by my side through it all, and my life has been electrified by the adventures of Sara and Fanny. Thank you for countless comforting conversations over pad Thai. Thank you for hilarious, unexpected text messages like,

"I was attacked by a pelican today, and no, I'm not drunk." Thank you for being my best friend.

To my loyal counterpart, Olive, who has literally been present for every keystroke of this book. *Seriously, you're staring at me right now.* Everyone thinks you're "just a cat," but I know better. I once almost lost my mind when the computer froze mid-recipe while I was writing this manuscript. You then chased an almond out from under the couch and sent me into uncontrollable laughter. You are truly one of a kind.

To my friend and local mentor, Judy Girard. I am forever indebted to you for your invaluable, thoughtful counseling and sound advice from day one. Over coffee we once chatted about how it was part of *your* life's path to help young women find their way. I can say without a doubt that your reassuring words of wisdom have steered me in the right direction and soared my ambitions to new heights. Just like my parents, you have believed in me from the start and reminded me to always be myself. It has led me here, and you are an irreplaceable rock on *my* path. I am so honored to have you in my life.

To each of you reading these words, those I know well and not at all, this book is for you. Thank you to my friends—near, far, old, and new—for being a part of who I am. Thank you for your encouragement, your enthusiasm, and your praise. What a divine fortune it is to have so many Fanny fans. We've got an exciting road ahead of us. Buckle your spatulas.

Index

31192020970446